SYMPHONY
OF LIFE

SYMPHONY
OF LIFE

A new spiritual anthology compiled by

Anna Jeffery

DIADEM BOOKS

Symphony of Life

Published by Diadem Books

For information, please contact:

Diadem Books
Mews Cottage
The Causeway
KENNOWAY
The Kingdom of Fife
KY8 5JU

www.diadembooks.com

Front cover design largely based on photographic artwork by Roger Gilroy.

ISBN: 978-1-907294-11-2

For Michael:
my dearest friend,
lover of music, companion on the Way

Contents

... the mighty symphony which
fills the universe to which our lives are destined to
make their tiny contribution and which is the self-expression
of the Eternal God.

From *The Spiritual Life*
Evelyn Underhill

All life is music, wherein is set all measures and all tones. We are building up a symphony of life – a symphony to God and higher and higher will we reach until we catch the melody of the angels.

From *The Gold of Dawn*
Source unknown

Music is a moral law. It gives a soul to the universe,
wings to the mind,
flight to the imagination, a charm to sadness, gaiety and life to
everything. It is the essence of order, and leads to all
that is good, just
and beautiful, of which it is the invisible, but
nevertheless dazzling,
passionate, and eternal form.

Plato

Foreword

"Music is a strange thing; I would almost say it is a miracle, for it stands half way between spirit and matter: we do not know what music is: it is part of the world of mystery." So wrote Heinrich Heine and there have always been those who have recognised something of the transcendent about music and its composition. "Mozart", wrote Goethe, "is a human incarnation of the divine creative power." And he went on to write: "I have my own particular sorrows, loves, delights and you have yours. But sorrow, gladness, yearning, hope, love, belong to all of us in all times and all places. Music is the only means whereby we feel these emotions in their universality, for music is the common language of all humanity." So it is entirely appropriate that Anna Jeffery should present this wonderful anthology in the context of a musical theme.

It might be thought that a writer who compiles an anthology of spiritual wisdom is one who lives an untroubled life spent in the peace of the library and the calm of the cloister. If this was ever true of anyone it is most certainly not true of Anna who in her own life has had to confront formidable challenges, both physical and spiritual. There can be no doubt that the contents of this book helped her to live through some long slow movements and alarming crescendos and to do so with quite amazing faith and courage.

What this magnificent book has done for her it can do for you.

Alex Wedderspoon
Dean Emeritus
Guildford

August 2009

About the Editor

Anna Jeffery lives in Surrey with her architect husband Michael. She has a background of health service, school and church administration combined with a deeply held Christian faith; for many years she has been aware of an inner drive to help others come to that same shared faith.

In 1992 she launched Cultural Country Retreats, a national network of retreats 'with a difference' primarily for those on the fringe of the church who were seeking a spiritual dimension to their lives. These were held at some of the finest retreat houses in the UK, providing a cultural and rural framework within which spiritual thought and reflection could take place. The blend of rural setting, musical input (classical music festivals) and buildings of rich historical interest, together with the spiritual dimension, enriched the lives of all who participated. The retreats, which ran for many years, are currently being restructured.

Unusually creative, she is driven by a desire to help those preoccupied with material wealth and values, seek a deeper, more meaningful approach to life which she believes is the only stabilising factor in this increasingly violent and unstable world – the only wealth worth seeking.

Recently retired, she is currently working on the establishment of Soul-Food Groups (a network of discussion groups based on the five books in the Vision series, edited by Rev William Sykes, former Chaplain of University College, Oxford); she also works in a voluntary capacity with local charities.

Symphony of Life is Anna's second book. Her first – *Five Gold Rings* – was published by Darton, Longman & Todd in 2003.

Introduction

The Oxford Dictionary defines the word "Symphony" as "**harmony of sounds**" – thus in this *Symphony of Life* are presented many different **sounds** or **pieces** from many different sources – each of which alone cannot produce the rich harmony of a full orchestra but together – each sounding a different note of spirituality in its own time, blended in perfect harmony, forms the rich tone of a full orchestra – under the baton of the principal conductor – God Himself.

After all, Life surely *is* a symphony with ups and downs – dark phrases and lighter ones with glorious uplands of magical harmonies that lift the spirit to realms of the ethereal; this concept forms the structure to what I hope will be an uplifting and unusual anthology. Perhaps, technically, symphonies are not usually composed in this format but let us say it is the anthologer's licence!

In the same way that a conductor cannot force members of the orchestra to follow his baton, so God cannot force us to follow Him. But those who do – find the resultant harmony in their lives to be truly inspirational – more so than the discord heard by those who reject a valid belief system.

This is an anthology of other men's insights, other men's inspirations – and we need all that they give in order that we might make sense of those difficult, obscure parts of the symphony when God seems silent – or the storm clouds gather – or the desert unending. We need their awareness, their perception, their understanding so that we too can perceive, understand, pick up the theme of the symphony in the still, silent centre of our souls. Then and only then are we lifted into the heights of inexpressible joy as we become aware of God immanent and transcendent.

I have compiled this *Symphony of Life* because it is a book I would love to find on any bookshelf – a book which includes pieces that other anthologies leave out and which leaves out much that they usually leave in! It is a book to inspire at a time when many have questions but few have answers, a time when our search for spirituality deepens, when many doubt and many more despair, a time when all of us face an uncertain future – this book sets out to lead the wary, encourage the doubtful, calm the fearful; it offers those hungry for reassurance – hope, certainty and surely a glimpse of the Divine.

Anna Jeffery
Guildford
August 2009

Prelude

Beginning / early awareness of God

Editor's Introduction

Our Prelude begins by drawing us into
the mystery that is an awakening awareness of God. It is beautifully
expressed by Charles Handy in **"The Mystery of the Universe"** (p. 8) where
he
asks pertinent questions:

- What keeps us Good?
- Whence comes our Energy?
- Could it be chance?
- Or is there Something?

Yes indeed, there is – summed up so beautifully by Richard Harries (p. 9)
"Questioning Belief" – Because God IS real and we are spiritual beings there
is a restlessness about us which will never be satisfied with a purely physical
existence.

We must let Bernard Ullathorne (p. 12) have the last word:

"Nothing in this world is so marvellous as the transformation
that a soul undergoes when the light of faith descends upon the light of
reason."

A definition of the word *retreat*

To go on retreat is not to "opt out" of one's social responsibility or to treat the life of the monastery or enclosed order as superior to that of the city streets. Retreats are a sharpening of our perception, a purifying of vision, a training programme for the spirit. In retreat we seek to be able to go on serving the world with renewed strength without being dominated or swallowed up by it. So rest and activity both have a place there…

A private retreat is one in which the individual organizes his own programme of prayer and works out his own timetable. The purpose is to deepen and nourish the life of the spirit by withdrawal and concentrated attention…

To withdraw even for a short time, into solitude is to disengage oneself from the oppression of words. Our age is one which is marked and disfigured by the corruption and dehumanising of language. We live under the constant onslaught of words from advertisements and from propaganda and the clichés and slogans of the consumer technocracies. Words by the million wash over us in a wave of meaninglessness. But the recovery of meaning and of resistance to this oppression derives from the practice of inner silence…

As St. Anthony expressed it, "Who sits in solitude and is quiet has escaped from three wars: hearing, speaking, seeing: yet against one thing shall he continually battle: that is his own heart." The battle in the heart, as we have seen, is more important than external battles, for the heart is the centre of life.

Kenneth Leech
From *True Prayer*

Is there not much more mystery in the relations of man to man than we generally recognize? None of us can truly assert that he really knows someone else, even if he has lived with him for years. Of that which constitutes our inner life we can impart even to those most intimate with us only fragments; the whole of it we cannot give nor would they be able to comprehend it. We wander through life together in semi-darkness in which none of us can distinguish exactly the features of his neighbour, only from time to time through some experience we have of our companion, or through some remark that he passes he stands for a moment close to us as though illuminated by a flash of lightning. Then we see him as he really is. After that we again walk on together in the darkness, perhaps for a long time and try in vain to make out our fellow-traveller's features.

To this fact, that we are each a secret to the other, we have to reconcile ourselves. To know one another cannot mean to know everything about each other; it means to feel mutual affection and confidence and to believe in one another. To analyse others – unless it be to help back to a sound mind someone who is in spiritual or intellectual confusion – is a rude commencement for there is a modesty of soul which we must recognise just as we do that of the body. The soul too has its clothing of which we must not deprive it and no one has the right to say to another: "Because we belong to each other as we do I have a right to know all your thoughts." In this matter giving is the only valuable process; it is only giving that stimulates. Impart as much as you can of your spiritual being to those who are on the road with you and accept as something precious what comes back to you from them....only those who respect the personality of others can be of real use to them.

I think therefore that no one should compel himself to show to others more of his inner life than he feels it natural to show. We can do no more than let others judge for themselves what we inwardly and really are and do the same ourselves with them. The one essential thing is that we strive to have light in ourselves. Our strivings will be recognised by others and when people have light in themselves it will shine out from them. Then we get to know each other as we walk together in the darkness without needing to pass our hands over each other's faces or to intrude into each other's hearts.

Albert Schweitzer
From *The Mystery of Man*

Why don't we die?
So much of life is worry, toil and tears
Why do we strive so busily to stay alive?
Why not just die?

What is Beauty made of?
We love the beauty in a sunset, a painting or a face
We know it's beauty when we see it, but who can say
What makes it so?

And then there's Joy
How good it is to laugh, to sing, to dance,
To see the eyes of children smile – but who
Invented Joy?

Or what of Love?
Why *should* we care for others, or put another first?
Why need the love of others to be whole ourselves?
A strange thing Love.

Whence comes our Energy?
So many strive each day to build a better world,
Putting heart and body to a stringent daily test,
Why *do* they bother?

What keeps us Good?
When the way ahead is snared with tempting traps
Like sloth and gluttony, or selfishness and greed.
Whence comes our virtue?

Could it be chance?
We all are just a random mix of genes
Our feelings chemistry, our bodies particles in flight.
Is it all luck?

Or is there something?
Some force or reason, some point behind it all
Something that hounds us on, for each to find
A Spirit and a Truth?

Charles Handy
From *Waiting for the Mountain to Move*

There is a basic, inescapable contradiction at the heart of religion. Like marriage, we cannot live with it and we cannot live without it. God is the supreme reality, from whom moment by moment our being flows. To live at one with him is Life. To turn our backs on him, through indifference or rebellion, brings disaster. We are dependent upon God as we are upon the air we breathe or the ground we walk on. To live in radical dependence upon the ground of our being is simply to acknowledge reality. To fail to acknowledge reality skews the whole of human society. Saints are those who consciously and consistently live out this reality. Yet religion is a defining fact in some of the most brutal and insoluble conflicts on the earth.

This contradiction is inescapable and ineradicable. Because God is real and we are spiritual beings, there is a restlessness about us which will never be satisfied with a purely physical existence. We look for some great cause to give ourselves to, whether communism, nationalism, sport or the arts. And because we are flawed, we are always in danger of attributing infinite values to that which is less than infinite, of giving absolute loyalty to what is less than absolute; in short, of committing idolatry.

So religion is here to stay. It will not go away.

Millions and millions of people believe and believe passionately; and they believe in the particular religion which has shaped and nurtured them. It is this religion which, for all its faults, gives meaning and purpose to their lives, which inspires idealism and encourages compassion.

Rt Rev Richard Harries
From *Questioning Belief*

We live in a period in which it is not possible to talk meaningfully about God. People still try to do so of course but they gradually become aware of difficulties which would not have troubled our ancestors. They find they must do it with a wryness and humour which is a kind of apology for slipping into a vocabulary that is not truly acceptable. Or they find they must do it with an excessive fervour which somehow embarrasses and alienates those with whom they are trying to hold a conversation. Or they find that they are searching for words and ideas outside the traditional field of theology in an attempt to make what they say meaningful for themselves and others.

The problem is not that we have ceased to want to talk about numinous experiences. The groping to do so goes on and there seems no good reason that it should cease so long as there are men left on earth. We need to know if there is meaning in the universe, to know what sort of creatures we are ourselves. We may need some knowledge about the kind of world it is to have any sort of coherent moral system...we cannot live without any sense of meaning in our lives.

Over the years, there seems as if there is a loss of meaning, possibly brought about by the growth of conurbations, disappearance of smaller communities, collapse of the extended family, increased mobility of the population, the disintegrative effect of two gigantic world wars in the first half of the century with the loss of huge numbers of young (and older men) with all that they might have brought to thought and stability; under such stresses people became aware that they are less meaningful for others and lacking this affirmation feel less meaningful to themselves. It may be that this loss has made us all less capable of maintaining traditional attitudes to religion or it may be that the loss of traditional attitudes has made us less able to maintain social cohesion. Whatever the origin it does appear we have lost something precious to our sense of well-being.

Is it recoverable and if so, in what form?
Is the church as it has been still an adequate vessel for the kind of meaning we are seeking?

What seems likely is that instead of being *the* source of spiritual enlightenment in the west, the church will become *one of a number of sources* and men will feel freer to search for what they need among a number of traditions as it is recognised that all men are engaged upon a spiritual search; all men are striving for wholeness.

Monica Furling
From *The End of Our Exploring*

Nothing in this world is so marvellous as the transformation that a soul undergoes when the light of faith descends upon the light of reason.

W.Bernard Ullathorne
From *Endowments of Man*

Be patient with everyone, but above all be patient with thyself. I mean, do not be disheartened by your imperfections, but instantly set about remedying them – every day begin the task anew.

St.Francis de Sales

A journey of a thousand miles must begin with a single step.

The way of Lao-Tzu
Taoism

Take my life, and let it be
Consecrated Lord to Thee.
Take my moments and my days,
Let them flow in ceaseless praise.
Take my hands and let them move
At the impulse of Thy love.
Take my feet and let them be
Swift and beautiful for Thee.

Take my voice, and let me sing
Always, only, for my King.
Take my lips, and let them be
Filled with messages from Thee.
Take my silver and my gold;
Not a mite would I withhold.
Take my intellect, and use
Every power as Thou shalt choose.

Take my will, and make it Thine;
It shall be no longer mine.
Take my heart, it is Thine own;
It shall be Thy royal throne.
Take my love, my Lord, I pour
At Thy feet its treasure store.
Take myself, and I will be
Ever, only, all for Thee.

Frances R.Harvergal

Thank God every morning when you get up that you have something to do which must be done, whether you like it or not. Being forced to work, and forced to do your best, will breed in you temperance, self-control, diligence, strength of will, content, and a hundred other virtues which the idle never know.

Charles Kingsley

Like a painting it is set before one,
But less brittle, ageless; these colours,
Are renewed daily with variations
Of light and distance that no painter
Achieves or suggests. Then there is movement,
Change, as slowly the cloud bruises
Are healed by sunlight, or snow caps
A black mood; but gold at evening
To cheer the heart. All through history
The great brush has not rested,
Nor the paint dried; yet what eye,
Looking coolly or, as we now,
Through the tears' lenses, ever saw
This work and it was not finished?

R.S. Thomas
The View from the Window

Now if it is these moments of recognition and awareness that change our minds and change our lives, if these can be the true turning points of human history, then something of enormous power must be at work in such commonplace experiences. One might say that a flash of recognition has a higher voltage than a flash of lightning, that the power that makes us suddenly aware is the secret of all evolution and the spark that sets off most revolutions.

But what is this force which causes me to see in a way in which I have not seen? What makes a landscape or a person or an idea come to life for me and become a presence towards which I surrender myself? I recognise, I respond, I fall in love, I worship – yet it was not I who took the first step. In every such encounter there has been an anonymous third party who makes the introduction, acts as a go-between, makes two beings aware of each other, sets up a current of communication between them. What is more, this invisible go-between does not simply stand between us but is activating each of us from inside.

John V. Taylor
From: *The Go-Between God*

The Christian vision...is a coherent one; it does not just illuminate a few isolated phenomena, but suffuses with meaning the entirety of evolution and the whole human existence, even on a day-to-day level.

M. Scott Peck
From *What Return can I make?*
Dimensions of the Christian Experience

Silence is one of the best preparations for communion with God and for the reception of inspiration and guidance. Silence itself of course has no magic. It may be sheer emptiness, absence of words or noise or music. It may be an occasion for slumber. But it may be an intensified pause, a vitalised hush, a creative quiet, an actual moment of mutual and reciprocal correspondence with God. The actual meeting of man with God and God with man is the very crown and culmination of what we can do with our human life here on earth.

Rufus M. Jones
Religious Society of Friends

Prayer is our humble answer to the inconceivable surprise of living. It is all we can offer in return for the mystery by which we live.

Abraham Joshua Heschel

Chesterton said the worst moment in the life of an atheist was when his heart was overflowing with thankfulness and he had no one to thank. So sometimes gratitude alone may make one feel it would be good to explore this, begin to take it seriously, to see what happens... then I've talked about the call, the sense that somehow there is a Thou in all this universe, it isn't just an **IT** and I feel myself **ADDRESSED.** It is as if one were given the end of a golden string – a clue – and then it is up to you to decide whether it is worth following up. It may lead nowhere. But on the other hand, it has a sense of value, a sense of ultimate importance: it's worth following to see what you find.

Gerald Priestland
From *The Case Against God*

Behind all questions of human relations lies the ultimate question of man's existence, whether there is beyond all his strivings a Goodness and Perfection in the universe itself towards which he may climb and a Love in which he may trust, or whether he has nothing to rely on except his own strength and wisdom and can find no value in the world that is not of his own making. The purpose which dominates the life of society today is the ambition of man to transform the world, society and himself by means of his science and technics. In so far as this endeavour is the exercise of the freedom and responsibility with which man has been endowed by the Creator, there is no reason to quarrel with it. But it makes the whole difference whether he engages in the task in self-sufficiency and pride or in the knowledge that he is a partner with God in His work of creation. If man is in truth a created being, intended to live and work in partnership with God, he does violence to his essential nature when he forgets that fact, and his efforts are likely to meet with repeated and multiplying frustration unless they are redeemed and purified by the humility that is born of worship.

J.H. Oldham
From *Florence Allshorn and the Story of St. Julian's*

Ring out the thousand wars of old
Ring in the thousand years of peace.
Ring out the old, ring in the new,
Ring, happy bells, across the snow:
The year is going, let him go;
Ring out the false, ring in the true.
Ring out old shapes and foul disease;
Ring out the narrowing lust of gold;
Ring out the thousand wars of old,
Ring in the thousand years of peace.

Ring in the valiant man and free,
The larger heart, the kindlier hand;
Ring out the darkness of the land;
Ring in the Christ that is to be.

Alfred Lord Tennyson
1809-92

...[there] are those sensitive spirits in whom we can see a great spreading of consciousness, awareness, a clear intensity of vision, a steady control over circumstances. The mind is not screwed down so tightly to the work-a-day world but has become attuned to a deeper rhythm. They have the victory of a forward moving spirit. They have found that which is at the heart of every prophet's vision, which every artist struggles to communicate, *and which all great music tries to utter – the rich yet simple revelation of God.*

J.H. Oldham
From *Florence Allshorn and the Story of St.Julian's*

We don't really direct our lives unaided and unobstructed. Our being is subject to all the chances of life. There are so many things we are capable of, that we could be or do. The potentialities are so great that we never, any of us, are more than one-fourth fulfilled...

Katherine Anne Porter
From *Conversations*

I believe that in each life there is a spiritual line, an upward curve, and all that adheres to and strengthens this line is our real life – the rest is but as chaff falling from us as our souls progress...

Isadora Duncan
From *My Life*

This astonishing sky, the desolation of colossal mountains, the fretwork of clouds and grey peaks, the eternal snows, the solemn silence of the wastes, the absence of any sound, any living being, any vegetation and above all of a great city that might recall the world of men: all combined to conjure up an image of a new world or to transport the spectator to primitive times. There was a moment when I could believe I was witnessing the birth of creation from the lap of chaos.

Henriette D'Angeville
From *My Ascent of Mont Blanc*

The Realization that every act, every word, every thought of ours not only influences our environment but mysteriously forms an integral part of the Universe, fits into it as if by necessity, in the very moment we do or say or think it, is an overwhelming and even shattering experience.

If we only knew deeply, absolutely, that our smallest act, our smallest thought, has such far-reaching effects; setting forces in motion; reaching out to the galaxy; how carefully we would act and speak and think. How precious life would become in its integral oneness.

Irina Tweedie
From *Chasm of Fire*

I give you the end of a golden string;
Only wind it into a ball,
It will lead you in at heaven's gate,
Built in Jerusalem's wall.

William Blake

Sometimes something breaks suddenly into our lives and upsets their normal pattern and we have to begin to adjust ourselves to a new kind of existence. This experience may come, as it came to me, through nature and poetry, or through art or music; or it may come through the adventure of flying or mountaineering or of war; or it may come simply through falling in love, or through some accident, an illness, the death of a friend, a sudden loss of fortune. Anything which breaks through the routine of daily life may be the bearer of this message to the soul. But however it may be, it is as though a veil has been lifted and we see for the first time behind the façade which the world has built round us. Suddenly we know that we belong to another world, that there is another dimension to existence. It is impossible to put what we have seen into words; it is something beyond all words which has been revealed.

There can be few people to whom such an experience does not come at some time, but it is easy to let it pass and to lose its significance. The old habits of thought reassert themselves; our world returns to its normal appearance and the vision which we have seen fades away. But these are the moments when we really come face to face with reality; in the language of theology they are moments of grace. We see our life for a moment in its true perspective in relation to eternity. We are freed from the flux of time and see something of the eternal order which underlies it. We are no longer isolated individuals in conflict with our surroundings; we are parts of a whole, elements in a universal harmony.

This, as I understand it, is the "golden string" of Blake's poem. It is the grace which is given to every soul, hidden under the circumstances of our daily life and easily lost if we choose not to attend to it. To follow up the vision which we have seen, to keep it in mind when we are thrown back again on the world, to live in its light and to shape our lives by its law, is to wind the string into a ball and to find our way out of the labyrinth of life. ...

Bede Griffiths
From The Prologue to *The Golden String*

I think it's important that faith starts with reason, and that's not reason in some narrow sense of just doing logic. It's all in the way that human beings try to make sense of their experience, and that's through philosophy, but it's also through art and poetry and plays and so on. Faith embraces all the sense that we have of the meaning of our lives but leads us beyond that to the ultimate meaning which is God.

Father Timothy Radcliffe
from *Belief*
Edited by Joan Bakewell

Our treasure lies in our inner life. It is our inner life which affects our perception of the world and determines our actions and reactions to it.

... in religious language this inner life is called "the soul", and the art of knowing it, healing it and harmonizing its forces is called spirituality.

Religion should encourage us to become more aware of this inner life and should teach us how to befriend it, for it is the source of our strength and storehouse of our wisdom.

Gerard Hughes
From *God of Surprises*

"I want to prepare you, to organise you for life..."

"Live all you can – as complete and full a life as you can find – do as much as you can for others. Read, work, enjoy, love and help as many souls – do all this. Yes, but remember: be alone, be remote, be away from the world. Then you will be near God!"

"I want you to hold very clearly the *otherness* of God, and the littleness of men..."

"Man is both of, and not of, this world; the soul lives in two worlds – hence the tension..."

"Religion is not man-made: it is immense: it comes from outside..."

"I want to write plainly and fully... about the problem of evil, the power of evil in a world ruled by an omnipotent God the source of all good; we never get rid of this problem. We can only minimise it." . . .

"God will have seen that far more happiness than misery would have been brought into existence by the creation of beings capable of sin; and he would have preferred to bring that happiness into being, even accompanied by this misery."

"Never try to begin to help people or influence them, till they ask, but wait for them. The souls to be helped are mostly at quite different stages from our own... one should wait in silence for those who do not open out to us, who are not intended, perhaps, ever to be helped by us – except by our prayers. We must be tolerant and patient, too, with those we can, and ought to help."

"God has never left the world in complete and groping darkness; all religions contain *some* light from God."

Letters from Baron Friedrich von Hugel to a Niece
Extracts from The Introduction:
Edited by Gwendolen Greene

There cannot be imagined a deeper gulf between men than that which divides those who are convinced that in meeting the present crisis in human existence men have to rely solely and exclusively on resources within themselves – from those who believe that there is a meaning in life which men do not create but find, that there is an end which they are meant to live for, a goodness to which they may respond in surrender and self-commitment and a love in which they may absolutely trust.

J.H. Oldham
Introduction to Chapter 6
Nurslings of Immortality by Rayner C.Johnson

Disclosure

Prayer is like watching for the
Kingfisher. All you can do is
Be where he is likely to appear, and
Wait.
Often, nothing much happens;
There is space, silence and
Expectancy.
No visible sign, only the
Knowledge that he's been there,
And may come again.
Seeing or not seeing cease to matter,
You have been prepared.
But sometimes, when you've almost
Stopped expecting it,
A flash of brightness
Gives encouragement.

Ann Lewin
(Watching for the Kingfisher
Canterbury Press)

We need not think of the task which God has in store for us in terms of some great act or achievement of which everyone will know.

It may be to fit a child for life; it may be at some crucial moment to speak that word and exert that influence which will stop someone ruining a life; it may be to do some quite small job superlatively well; it may be something which will touch the lives of many by our hands, our voices or our minds. The fact remains that God is preparing us by all the experiences of life for something and we must not fail in rising to the challenge when it comes.

William Barclay

1st Movement: Allegro moderato

(normal / constant / progressing – the steady influence of God)

Introduction to First Movement

Here a myriad voices speak of the
steady, constant influence of God in our lives – which streams forth in an
unstoppable torrent – as in a waterfall.
This First Movement sets out the foundation of our faith with George
Herbert's spectacular words on Prayer (p. 58) describing it as

" …the Church's banquet – heart
in pilgrimage – gladness of the best – the soul's blood – land of spices –
something understood."

What could possibly follow that? But many do – R.S.Thomas (p. 60)
describes

The Moor:

"like a church to me" where "no prayers said – but stillness of the heart's
passions – praise enough" and so our First Movement builds – with so much
to make even the hardest of hearts stop – pause and listen to all that
makes one mindful of God's splendour. Here let Neville Ward (p. 64) write
as we cannot:

"It is at once by poetry and by penetrating beyond it, by music and
by penetrating beyond it, that the soul catches a glimpse of
the splendour on the other side of the grave
and when an exquisite poem brings tears to the eyes, these tears are no proof
of excessive pleasure. They are rather the witness of a nature exiled
in the imperfect which longs to seize immediately… the paradise revealed
to it."

The Movement builds and we feel gratitude to gifted men such as Rabbi Jonathan Sacks for setting out so clearly (p. 74) the purpose of our lives…
and to
Evelyn Underhill (p. 57) for proclaiming

"Love… offers us all that it has and demands from us all that we can give."

A place where tears are understood
  where I can cry …
A place where my spirit can take wing
  and I can fly…
A place where my questions can be asked
  where I can seek…
A place where my feelings can be heard
  where I can speak….
A place where I can be accepted as I am
  where I can be…
A place where I can learn and grow
  where I can be me…

A special place – *source unknown*

Time itself is neutral; it can be used either destructively or constructively. More and more I feel that the people of ill will have used time much more effectively than have the people of good will. We have to repent in this generation not merely for the hateful word and actions of the bad people, but for the appalling silence of the good people. Human progress never rolls in on wheels of inevitability; it comes through the tireless efforts of women and men willing to be co-workers with God, and without this hard work, time itself becomes the ally of the forces of social stagnation. We must use time creatively, in the knowledge that the time is always ripe to do the right.

Martin Luther King – *writing from the darkness of a prison cell.*

Do all the good you can
By all the means you can
In all the ways you can
In all the places you can
To all the people you can
As long as ever you can

John Wesley

The joy of life is living it and doing things of worth,
In making bright and fruitful all the barren spots of earth.
In facing odds and mastering them and rising from defeat,
And making true what once was false, and what was
       bitter, sweet.
For only he knows perfect joy whose little bit of soil
Is richer ground than what it was when he began to toil.

Anon.

Only when we feel that through all our vicissitudes some unfathomable purpose runs, and that by meeting life nobly and courageously we can cooperate in the fulfilment of that purpose, do we find peace.

Alice Hegan Rice
Happiness Road

Faithfulness is consecration in overalls. It is the steady acceptance and performance of the common duty and immediate task without any reference to personal preferences — because it is there to be done and so is a manifestation of the will of God.

Faithfulness means continuing quietly with the job we have been given, in the situation where we have been placed; not yielding to the restless desire for change. It means tending the lamp quietly for God without wondering how much longer it has got to go on. Steady unsensational driving, taking good care of the car. A lot of the road to heaven has to be taken at thirty miles per hour. It means keeping everything in your charge in good order for love's sake...

Faithfulness is the quality of the friend, refusing no test and no trouble, loyal, persevering; not at the mercy of emotional ups and downs or getting tired when things are tiresome. In the interior life of prayer, faithfulness points steadily to God and His purposes, away from self and its preoccupations.

Evelyn Underhill
The Fruits of the Spirit

The supreme test of goodness is not in the greater but in the smaller incidents of our character and practice; not what we are when standing in the searchlight of public scrutiny, but when we reach the firelight flicker of our homes; not what we are when some clarion call rings through the air, summoning us to fight for life and liberty, but our attitude when we are called to sentry duty in the grey morning, when the watchfire is burning low. It is impossible to be our best at the supreme moment if character is corroded and eaten into by daily inconsistency, unfaithfulness, and besetting sin.

F.B. Meyer
Our Daily Walk

Live not as though there were a thousand years ahead of you. Fate is at your elbow, make yourself good while life and power are still yours.

Marcus Aurelius
Meditations

We must accept finite disappointment but we must never lose infinite hope.

Martin Luther King

The greatest attainment in the world of humanity is nearness to God. Every lasting glory, honour, grace, and beauty which comes to man comes through nearness to God. All the Prophets and apostles longed and prayed for nearness to the Creator... Nearness to God is possible through devotion to Him, through entrance into the Kingdom and service to humanity; it is attained by unity with mankind and through loving-kindness to all; it is dependent upon investigation of truth, acquisition of praiseworthy virtues, service in the cause of universal peace and personal sanctification. In a word, nearness to God necessitates sacrifice of self, severance and the giving up of all to Him. Nearness is likeness.

Baha'i Faith
Promulgation of Universal Peace

Purity is not innocence; it is much more. Purity is the outcome of sustained spiritual sympathy with God. We have to grow in purity. The life with God may be right, and the inner purity remain unsullied, and yet every now and again the bloom on the outside may be sullied. God does not shield us from this possibility, because in this way we realize the necessity of maintaining the vision by personal purity. If the spiritual bloom of our life with God is getting impaired in the tiniest degree, we must leave off everything and get it put right. Remember that vision depends on character – the pure in heart see God.

Oswald Chambers
My Utmost for His Highest

My life is an influence on every life mine touches. Whether I realize it or not, I am responsible and accountable for that influence.

Ron Baron

Withdraw into yourself and look. And if you do not find yourself beautiful as yet, do as does the creator of a statue that is to be made beautiful; he cuts away here, he smoothes there, he makes this line lighter, this other purer, until he has shown a beautiful face upon his statue. So do you also; cut away all that is excessive, straighten all that is crooked, bring light to all that is shadowed, labour to make all glow with beauty, and do not cease chiselling your statue until there shall shine out on you the godlike splendour of virtue, until you shall see the final goodness surely established in the stainless shrine.

Plotinus

If anyone can control his tongue, it proves that he has perfect control over himself in every other way. We can make a large horse turn around and go wherever we want by means of a small bit in his mouth. And a tiny rudder makes a huge ship turn wherever the pilot wants it to go, even though the winds are strong.

So also the tongue is a small thing, but what enormous damage it can do. A great forest can be set on fire by one tiny spark. And the tongue is a flame of fire. ...the tongue can be set on fire by hell itself; and can turn our whole lives into a blazing flame of destruction and disaster.

James 3.2-6
New Testament

Hope is
A resting place
Beside
Life's climbing way
Where
We can pause
To check
Our trusted maps.
We may not stay
Still less expect
Such sure support
When we forget
To pray
With those
Like us confined
By what
The best guides
Say

David J. Harding
A Resting Place

Prayer, the Church's banquet, Angels' age,
    God's breath in man returning to his birth,
The soul in paraphrase, heart in pilgrimage,
    The Christian plummet, sounding heaven and earth;
Engine against the Almighty, sinner's tower,
    Reversed thunder, Christ-side-piercing spear,
The six-days' world transposing in an hour,
    A kind of tune, which all things hear and fear;
Softness, and peace, and joy, and love, and bliss,
    Exalted manna, gladness of the best,
    Heaven in ordinary, man well drest,
The milky way, the bird of Paradise,
    Church-bells beyond the stars heard, the soul's
    blood,
The land of spices; something understood.

George Herbert
Prayer

Faith brings us back to the Why that must precede the How. Why do we work, build, strive? To create a world that gives dignity to the personal, that honours the image of God in the human frame...

Jonathan Sacks
Faith Found
From *Celebrating Life*

It was like a church to me.
I entered it on soft foot,
Breath held like a cap in the hand.
It was quiet.
What God was there made himself felt,
Not listened to, in clean colours
That brought a moistening of the eye,
In movement of the wind over grass.

There were no prayers said. But stillness
Of the heart's passions – that was praise
Enough; and the mind's cession
Of its kingdom. I walked on,
Simple and poor, while the air crumbled
And broke on me generously as bread.

R.S.Thomas
The Moor

Therefore, as you pray, expressing your aspirations and desires, you are exposing yourself to the ultimate reality – to God. You *are* talking to yourself of course, and so is the most devout man who says his prayers. But God is *in* you as well as above you – he is both immanent and transcendent. He does not live in the top left hand corner of your bedroom, nor is his presence confined to church. He is spirit, and he is within and around you, closer to you than the air you breathe. As you spell out your desires and think your wishes, you are talking to God, you *are* praying. God is within and around you. In him you live and move and have your being.

Reginald Cant
Canon of York
From *Christian Prayer*

...we have no right to call anyone 'ordinary' for each one of us is extraordinary, an ensouled body made in the divine likeness; and the real blindness, that culpable blindness of the spirit that can only be compared to living in the dark, is the failure to see the true value, the wonder and the mystery of every person you meet.

Michael Mayne
From *Pray, Love, Remember*

Let me be mindful of God's splendour,
not only in those quiet half hours
plucked from the day between sleeping and rising,
from the silent room on peaceful evenings,
    with books outspread.
But as I rush through the world,
race through that strident turbulence
of urgency and incidence,
let me so carry God's great glory
like a torch in my hand,
a sun in my face,
a flame in my heart,
that people may turn in their tracks,
feeling the warmth of it,
catching the light…

Virginia Thesiger
From *Let me be Mindful*

There is a point at which the mind finds it possible simply to rest in contentment with one or other of the forms of God's presence that are given us in this world... The looking at and resting in appreciated good is contemplation.

Wherever a man's mind has been uplifted, his temptations thwarted, his sorrows comforted, his resolutions strengthened... by the sight of purity, innocence, love or beauty...

In the experience of the arts (listening to music, looking at a picture) or when enjoying the view of a wide and various landscape or certain moments of tranquillity and happiness in the infinitely diverse experience of human love, the mind seems not to be doing anything at all, it is simply attending in quietness and joy to what is in front of it. It is this faculty of the mind to attend, without one thought giving way to another, that is the characteristic feature of contemplation. Practically everyone is familiar with it.

During the contemplation of a work of art or while listening to a piece of music, the effort to understand relaxes and the soul simply delights itself in the beauty which it divines...

It is at once by poetry and by penetrating beyond it, by music and by penetrating beyond it, that the soul catches a glimpse of the splendour on the other side of the grave and when an exquisite poem brings tears to the eyes, these tears are no proof of excessive pleasure. They are rather the witness of a nature exiled in the imperfect which longs to seize immediately... the paradise revealed to it.

J. Neville Ward
From *The Use of Praying*

The very familiarity of the world about us serves as a kind of cataract which blinds us to the sheer prodigality of God whose world of colours and sights and sounds ought to make us drunk with their beauty. And time and time again it is the artist – the poet – the painter – the musician – the novelist who sees beneath the surface of things to that deeper dimension of spirit and by their choice of words or notes of music or their use of paint or wood or stone, capture a truth about the mystery and wonder of life which cause us to catch our breath as, for a moment, we see with their eyes and share their vision.

Michael Mayne
From *Prayer for the Day*
BBC Radio

For merriment is the birthright of the young. But we can all keep it in our hearts as life goes on if we hold fast by the spirit that refuses to admit defeat; by the faith that never falters, by the hope that cannot be quenched.

King George VI
BBC Radio Broadcast, 1945

Love is the cosmic energy that flames from the constellations and is concealed in the abyss of the atom; is whispered by the Holy Spirit in the heart and placarded before men's eyes upon the Cross.

It offers us all that it has and demands from us all that we can give.

Evelyn Underhill
From *An anthology of the love of God*

Father, I have not given to myself the life that breathes in me; the origin of my power to act and to love are discovered in you. It is not my effort, nor the effort of anyone around me, that initiates this personal life that is mine. Nor can my anxiety add or take anything from its powerful movement. The flow of mind and heart, which is the experience of being alive, is pure gift; it comes into me, and I receive its mysterious energy, moment by moment, This gift of myself, this torrent of existence, comes pouring into me from you. I am receiving my life from your hands.

Reflecting on this gift, I am aware that there is a strange paradox hidden in it. On the one hand it is a free flow of opportunity and occasion so that my life is my own to form, out of my aspirations and desires. Life comes from you, but its shape and history is in my hands. Yet, on the other hand, my life comes to me from you with many outside and inside patterns that are not of my creating. You give me freedom, and at the same time give me the particular circumstances that surround that freedom. It is a though my life were at the same time entirely in your hands, and yet mysteriously given to me. It is not easy for me to understand.

What I believe and trust is, that in the freedom and the circumstances that are given to me, your loving, patient, and faithful concern is working all the time. My understanding may fail, but I believe that no circumstance is beyond the power of your love for me. I believe, too, that however blindly I may use my freedom, I am never beyond the power of your correcting hand. I not only receive my life from these hands of yours in circumstances and in freedom, I am cared for and guided by these same hands, wherever I am, and in whatever I do.

Picture Meditation
The Hands
House of the Resurrection
Mirfield

Our lives intertwine with one another's for our mutual learning, and we attract to ourselves those people and experiences we need to teach us whatever it is we need to learn...

Phyllis Krystal
From *Cutting The Ties that Bind*

Many people will walk in and out of your life,
But only true friends will leave footprints in your heart.

To handle yourself, use your head;
To handle others, use your heart.

Anger is only one letter short of danger.

If someone betrays you once, it is his fault;
If he betrays you twice, it is your fault.

Great minds discuss ideas;
Average minds discuss events;
Small minds discuss people.

One who loses money, loses much;
One who loses a friend, loses much, much more;
One who loses faith, loses all.

Beautiful young people are accidents of nature,
But beautiful old people are works of art.

Learn from the mistakes of others,
You can't live long enough to make them all yourself.

Yesterday is history.
Tomorrow is a mystery.
Today is a gift.

Eleanor Roosevelt

Education is about forming people who have the moral strength and spiritual depth to hold to a course and weather its ups and downs.

It is about forming people who know that economic competition is not more important than family life and love of neighbour, and that technical innovation is not more important than reverence for the beauty of creation. It is about forming people who, however academically and technically skilful, are not reduced to inarticulate embarrassment by the great questions of life and death, meaning and truth.

Church schools embody the truth that a context of firm principles suffused by faith and love is the best and right basis for learning and growing.

The Archbishop of Canterbury's definition of Education
From '*What Makes a Christian Schoool?*'
Michael Hepworth: *Daily Telegraph*, Wed 31st July 2002

...picture a saintly nun, in the eyes of the world unimportant and unknown, praying in a convent chapel. Yet from that obscure chapel are radiating currents of spiritual power which have influence far beyond the chapel walls.

This black figure knelt at the centre of reality and force and with the movements of her will and lips, controlled spiritual destinies for eternity. There ran out from this peaceful chapel lines of spiritual power that lost themselves in the distance, bewildering in their profusion and terrible in the intensity of their hidden power.

F.C.Happold
The Journey Inwards

Silence therefore is an integral part of prayer, for the words having done their job can drop away. Many public acts of worship fail to recognise this and are too relentlessly wordy; those leading public worship should allow space and silence for the spirit of prayer to move, without always trying to fence it in with verbiage. Congregations sometimes find the torrent of words in our liturgies to be exhausting. If we do use words they may in this context have to do more work than is expected of them in normal conversation or writing. Donald Allchin has written:

> *God can only speak to us, and we can only speak to God, and of God, in words which our human life has given to us. Because those words are always too small, too limited, too fragile to express the fullness of his being and his joy, we have to seek ways by which we may expand them, allow them to carry more weight, to hold together a greater wealth of meaning and experience than they would normally do. This is one reason why much of the language of faith and prayer is the language of poetry, language which is, we say, inspired.*

That is well said, and reminds us why so many people still want to use the well-tried resonant prayers of the past which have stronger tones and rhythms than some more recently composed prayers seem able to attain. Those stronger and evocative words are often the gateway to a productive silence in the presence of God.

Michael Adie
From *Held Together*

- Each of us is here for a purpose;
- Discerning that purpose takes time and honesty, knowledge of ourselves and knowledge of the world, but it is there to be discovered. Each of us has a unique constellation of gifts, an unreplicated radius of influence, and within that radius, be it as small as a family or as large as a state, we can be a transformative presence;
- Where *what we want to do* meets *what needs to be done*, that is where God wants us to be;
- Even the smallest good deed can change someone's life;
- It is not the honours we receive that matter but the honour we give;
- What counts is not how much wealth we make but how much of what we have, we share;
- Those who spend at least part of their lives in service of others are the most fulfilled and happiest people I know;
- There is no greater gift we can give our children than to let them see us sacrifice something for the sake of an ideal;
- No religion that persecutes others is worthy of respect, nor one that condemns others, entitled to admiration;
- We honour the world God created and called good by searching for and praising the good in others and the world;
- Nothing is gained by less-than-ethical conduct. We may gain in the short term but we will lose in the long, and it is the long term that counts;
- Moral health is no less important to the quality of a life than physical health;
- A word of praise can give meaning to someone's life;
- Putting others down, we diminish ourselves; lifting others, we lift ourselves;
- The world is a book in which our life is a chapter, and the question is whether others, reading it, will be inspired;
- Each situation in which we find ourselves did not happen by accident: we are here, now, in this place, among these people in these circumstances, so that we can do the act or say the word that will heal one of the fractures of the world;

- Few are the days when we cannot make some difference to the lives of others;
- Virtue does not have to be conspicuous to win respect;
- The best do good without thought of reward, understanding that to help others is a privilege even more than it is an opportunity;
- Cynicism diminishes those who practise it;
- It is not the most wealthy or powerful or successful or self-important who make the greatest difference or engender the greatest love;
- Pain and loneliness are forms of energy that can be transformed if we turn them outward, using them to recognize and redeem someone else's pain or loneliness;
- The people who are most missed are those who brought hope into our lives;
- The ability to give to others is itself a gift;
- We can make a difference, and it is *only* by making a difference that we redeem a life, lifting it from mere existence and endowing it with glory;
- Those who give to others are the closest we come to meeting the divine presence in this short life on earth;
- The best way of *receiving* a blessing is to *be* a blessing;
- If we listen carefully enough – and listening is an art that requires long training and much humility – we will hear the voice of God in the human heart telling us that there is work to do and that he needs us.

Jonathan Sacks
From *To Heal A Fractured World*

Why are some aware of that bottomless pool and their need to explore it, while others ignore or shy away from the inner life of the spirit? It would seem to have to do with human intelligence, the fact that we are driven to ask ultimate questions and see meaning in our lives. IQ (Intelligence Quotient) is a familiar concept: it describes our rational intelligence. EQ and SQ have now joined the dance, attempts to widen the understanding of how our brain functions. EQ is our emotional, SQ our spiritual, quotient. There is in each of us a mixture of both IQ and EQ in differing degrees, a dance of head and heart. We think and we feel, but emotions – love, anger, fear – are so strong that they usually carry the day. Stories, novels, film, theatre, art, poetry and music, all appeal to our emotions. While those with a high IQ tend to be intelligent, ambitious, productive, emotionally cool and usually introspective, those with a high EQ tend to be out-going and cheerful, socially at least, good at handling relationships, sympathetic and caring.

But what of this new fashionable concept of SQ? A high SQ will not necessarily make me religious, but it will mean that I have a sense of something greater and other than myself that adds meaning and value to my life. SQ describes the intelligence with which we address such questions, seeing our lives in this wider context. It allows us to be creative, flexible and self-aware, inspired with a vision of how things might be changed for the better and recognising our power to change them. IQ, EQ and SQ should work in harmony, though they may function separately, individuals being high in one and low in another.

My brain is the bridge between my outer and inner worlds and it brings us back to the mystery of how this thing called "consciousness" has the power, not only to *analyse* but also to *unite* the startling number of messages being fed into the brain's neural systems: shape, colour, sound, smell, touch. It seems that we all possess in some degree this higher order unitive intelligence that is SQ. It is essentially holistic so that those with low SQ find it hard to see beyond the immediate moment or place it within a wider framework of meaning, while those with high SQ make connections and recognise that the whole is always greater than the parts.

Michael Mayne
From *Learning to Dance*

The Spirit guides me here,
To meet upon this hill,
The outstretched arms, the wounded hands,
The love that finds me still.

In silence I am held,
Until my song takes flight
And breaking forth in golden notes
Fills heart and soul with light.

When I must leave this place
And face the world again
Good Saviour, from such holy ground
Come with me to the plain.

Consume my soul with fire,
Let love and peace fly free,
And at the end take all I am
And shape what I must be.

Christine McIntosh
Cathedral of the Isles, Cumbrae

There was a church, rising
Above green terraces of
Pleasing symmetry,
Surely too neat, too
Small to encompass much
Mystery.

Yet in that
Silent shell, in the golden
Brass-glow of candles,
God would touch
Careless souls, catch their
Hearts in a mesh of
Incandescent song, so that
Those who knelt there would
Pass through the veil of light
To the bright places beyond.

Christine McIntosh
Cathedral of the Isles, Cumbrae

After a memorably unpleasant night Mike and I followed an unnamed tributary that descended steeply into the crevasse-streaked maw of the Mill Glacier. The horizons which now opened to us in slow motion were awesome, a sprawling mass of rock and ice locked in suspended motion. This was the headwater of a *moving* ice-river. Constrictions caused by 15,000-foot-high mountains had formed, and were even now renewing savage whirlpools and mighty maelstroms of cascading pressure-ice. Huge open chasms leered from distant foot-hills and standing ice-waves reared up at the base of black truncated cliffs.

I found this canvas full of power and wonder and thanked God for this moment of being alive. Nothing else lived here nor ever had since the dinosaurs of Gondwanaland. No birds nor beasts nor the least bacteria survived. Only the deep roar of massive avalanche, the shriek and grind of splitting rock, the groan of shifting ice, and the music, soft or fierce, of the winds from a thousand valleys, moved to and fro across the eternal silence.

Ranulph Fiennes
The epic crossing of the Antarctic continent
From *Mind Over Matter*

We need society, and we need solitude also, as we need summer and winter, day and night, exercise and rest.   I thank heaven for a thousand pleasant and profitable conversations with acquaintances and friends; I thank heaven also, and not less gratefully, for thousands of sweet hours that have passed in solitary thought or labour, under the silent stars.

Society is necessary to give us our share and place in the collective life of humanity but solitude is necessary to the maintenance of the individual life. Society is to the individual what travel and commerce are to a nation, during which it develops its especial originality and genius.

The life of the perfect hermit, and that of those persons who feel themselves nothing individually, and have no existence but what they receive from others, are alike imperfect lives. The perfect life is like that of a ship of war which has its own place in the fleet and can share in its strength and discipline but can also go forth alone in the solitude of the infinite sea. We ought to belong to society, to have our place in it, and yet to be capable of a complete individual existence outside of it.

Which of the two is the grander, the ship in the disciplined fleet, arranged in order of battle, or the ship alone in the tempest, a thousand miles from land? The truest grandeur of the ship is in neither one nor the other but in the capacity for both. What would that captain merit who either had not seamanship enough to work under the eye of the admiral or else had not sufficient knowledge of navigation to be trusted out of range of signals?

I value society for the abundance of ideas that it brings before us, like carriages in a frequented street; but I value solitude for sincerity and peace and for the better understanding of the thoughts that are truly ours.

Philip Gilbert Hamerton
From *A Diary of Readings*
by John Baillie

Spirituality plays "an intrinsic role in our daily lives unbound by the strictures of an organised religion. Inner peace and compassion – threatened by today's materialistic culture – are sustained by spirituality. In turn, an awareness of our 'hidden seas' can lead to personal transformation and growth; to grow spiritually can allow one to become less concerned with superficial matters and develop a simpler personal vision. Rather than a retreat from the world this signifies an entry into the fullness of life…

We live in an age of instant gratification. Spirituality represents the opposite to this in giving no immediate feedback but requiring instead, a disciplined approach leading to long and silent growth. Its aim is to get beyond the self, to transcend it and thereby perceive the boundless possibilities and grandeur of what spirituality has to offer."

Sarah Anderson

Prayer... I knew that I did not understand it. I recognised its great power but I did not understand how a human being relates himself on so deep a level with God. It might be a wordless relationship, as I felt in the singing of the women. It could be made with words. I am sure it is no easier to pray than it is to create music or write a poem; it must be as hard to do as it is to build a bridge, or to discover a great scientific principle, or to heal the sick, or to understand another human being. It is surely as important as these to man in his search for his role in the universal scheme of things. That role? I hope to understand it better on this journey, somewhere.

To pray... It is so necessary and so hard. Hard not because it requires intellect or knowledge or a big vocabulary or special technics but because it requires of us humility. And that comes, I think, from a profound sense of one's brokenness, and one's need. Not the need that causes us to cry, "Get me out of this trouble, quick!" but the need that one feels every day of one's life – even though one does not acknowledge it – to be related to something bigger than one's self, something more alive than one's self, something older and something not yet born, that will endure through time.

Lilian Smith
From *The Journey*

Grant to us
Lord,
the royalty of inward happiness
and the serenity which comes from living close to thee.

Daily renew in us the sense of joy,
and let thy Spirit dwell in our hearts,
that we may bear about with us the infection of a good courage,
and may meet all life's ills and accidents
with gallant and high-hearted happiness,
giving thee thanks always for all things;

through Jesus Christ, our Lord.

From *A Prayer In The Life* (June, Marchioness of Aberdeen)
Selections from BBC Radio 4's Prayer for the Day
by James Whitbourn

Prayer is not just talking to oneself. Prayer is not even just talking to God. It is listening, seeing, understanding, doing. It is being spiritual farmers, harvesting a more enduring crop for the feeding of mankind. God has put man into a world where man must work and co-operate with the natural forces of life and growth around him. That has its spiritual counterpart too. In the realm of the Spirit man must also work and co-operate with the natural expressions of the Spirit that are around him. He must farm spiritually as well as materially. In prayer man is contributing in a way that he cannot yet measure for the health and wholeness of the collective mind, the group unconscious, the common psychic area in which we all swim. Fear and hatred grow at compound interest rates; so do love and peace. When we release the energy of fear into the world it is a real energy which affects and changes things. The same is true of love.

Gary Davies
From *Prayer*

"Talk about your definition of the soul. What do you believe the soul to be?"

"My understanding of 'soul' would be that it is the unseen, hidden dimension of the self; the place beneath or beside or above the mind and consciousness. To put it in imagistic terms and spatial terms, I think it is the field of presence or colour or light that suffuses and holds the body. The body is actually in the soul. Meister Eckhardt says that the soul has two faces. One faces towards the world, and the other faces towards the divine, where it receives as he says, 'the kiss of God.'

One of the most radical and subversive things I ever read is in the Latin writings of Meister Eckhardt. It is where he said there is a place in the soul that neither time, nor flesh, nor no created thing can touch. I think that's a radical and healing insight in a consumerist culture, where identity is reduced to biography. I think that makes a space for the eternal dimension of ourselves. "

John O'Donohue
in conversation with Joan Bakewell
From *Belief.*

(The spiritual life is).... "not only the subject matter of religion, but also the cause and goal of everything in human life that points beyond the world – great action, great music, great poetry, great art. *Our attention to it, or our neglect of it, makes no difference to the world, but it makes every difference to us.*

...all who are sensitive to beauty know the almost agonizing sense of revelation its sudden impact brings – the abrupt disclosure of the mountain summit, the wild cherry tree in blossom, the crowning moment of a great concerto, witnessing to another beauty beyond sense. And again, any mature person looking back on his or her own past life will be forced to recognize factors in that life which cannot be attributed to heredity, environment, opportunity, personal initiative or mere chance. The contact that proved decisive, the path unexpectedly opened, the other path closed, the thing we felt compelled to say, the letter we felt compelled to write. It is as if a hidden directive power, personal, living, free, were working through circumstances and often against our intention or desire, pressing us in a certain direction, and moulding us to a certain design...

...it implies that beneath the surface of life which generally contents us, there are unsuspected deeps and great spiritual forces that condition and control our small lives. Some people are... sensitive to the pressure of these forces. The rest of us easily ignore the evidence for this whole realm of experience, just because it is all so hidden and interior and we are so busy responding to obvious and outward things. ... When we take it seriously, it surely suggests that we are essentially spiritual as well as natural creatures and that therefore life in its fullness, the life that develops and uses all our capacities and fulfils all our possibilities, must involve correspondence not only with our visible and ever-changing (world) but also with our invisible and unchanging environment: the Spirit of all spirits, God in whom we live and move and have our being. The significance, the greatness of humanity, consists in our ability to do this. The meaning of our life is bound up with the meaning of the universe. ... And at once a new coherence comes into our existence, a new tranquillity and release... The people of our times are helpless, distracted and rebellious, unable to interpret what is happening and full of apprehension about what is to come, largely because they have lost this sure hold on the eternal which gives to each life meaning and direction and with meaning and direction gives steadiness".

Evelyn Underhill
What is the Spiritual Life?
From *The Spiritual Life.*

For she believed that we inhabit two worlds, one changing and the other unchanging, and that we could reach out towards the truths which lie beyond and above the reason with which we negotiate our way through our present life. As human beings, she believed, we have contact with many levels of reality.

Ann Loades
From *Evelyn Underhill's Life: A Pilgrimage of Hope*

When we talk of our development I fancy we mean little more than that we have changed with the changing world, and if we are writers or intellectuals, that our ideas have changed with the changing fashions of thought, and therefore not always for the better. I think that if any of us examines his life, he will find that most good has come to him from the few loyalties, and a few discoveries made many generations before he was born, which must always be made anew. These too may sometimes appear to come by chance, but in the infinite web of things and events chance must be something different from what we think it to be. To comprehend that is not given to us, and to think of it is to recognize a mystery, and to acknowledge the necessity of faith.

As I look back on the part of the mystery which is my own life, my own fable, what I am most aware of is that we receive more than we can ever give; we receive it from the past, on which we draw with every breath, but also – and this is a point of faith – from the Source of the mystery itself, by the means which religious people call Grace.

Edwin Muir
Mystery

If you were given the job of designing the perfect person I wonder how he would turn out.

Suppose for example instead of having to choose ten discs for your lonely desert island you had to choose an ideal companion, what qualities would you pick? I imagine we would all agree that the person must have a sense of humour. It would be terrible to live with someone incapable of laughing or sharing a joke. And this isn't just because people who can laugh with us are fun but because a sense of humour is essential for keeping things in perspective. People who can't laugh usually take themselves too seriously.

Then I would want someone with something up top. They wouldn't have to be highly educated but they would have to be capable of thinking for themselves.

We would of course want our companion to be kind but I think we would also agree that there is more to goodness than a warm heart; we would want them to have some steel to them, some guts. We don't want them to go to pieces or collapse in a heap of self-pity.

Then finally a quality that not everyone would value. I would design the ideal companion to be a holy person – a person who had a secret inner life that was deep and close to God. People who are labelled religious usually turn out to be the best or the worst people we know – this is because what is highest in human life can turn out terrible if it is even the slightest bit distorted. But if a person really is close to God they often seem to have a special something that is very attractive and very necessary for that desert island; for after all when you have made yourself comfortable and eaten your coconuts and swum and sunbathed – what is your life actually going to be about? A holy person would be a reminder that life is meant to be a spiritual journey into ever deeper layers of truth.

Richard Harries
Prayers of Grief and Glory
From *The Bridge is Love*
An anthology of Hope compiled by Elizabeth Basset

How would you define religion?

I define it in one of my books – *A Passionate Man* – when one of my characters said "Religion is an awakened sense of some great controlling force, an awareness that above or beyond there is not just freedom but fulfilment. And this awareness of power and possibility make us strive ever onwards morally, emotionally and spiritually."

Do you ever take time to look at God and if so, what do you see?

I don't take time to look. I take time to suspend myself a bit... I am conscious of a dimension – you could call it a spiritual dimension if you like... I don't want a blinding vision. I would rather have a mounting sense of reassurance, not so much for myself but for loved ones. I want to know they are going to be safe.

Safe from what?

Too many agonies and perils, too many disappointments. And although you can't shield anybody from disappointment, you can somehow help them to have the equipment to deal with it and I always hope some extra force will assist me in helping them...

Do you feel it's God's fault... that people feel at odds with themselves and with the world?

...I believe we have free will. Without question. The penalty of having free will is that you have to accept the consequences of the decisions you make using your free will. So you can't then, having made a choice, turn round and shake your fist at God and say "look what you've made me do."

One of the things about getting older is that you know the storm clouds. They'll always be there but they're not going to overwhelm you. They will pass a little. The sun will come out again…

Bel Mooney talking to Joanna Trollope
From *Devout Sceptics*: *Conversations on Faith and Doubt*

Most of us have collections of sayings we live by: whenever words fly up to me from a printed page, I intercept them instantly, knowing they are for me. I turn them over in my mind and cling to them hard.

David Grayson

Prayer is...an invisible emanation of man's worshipping spirit – the most powerful form of energy that one can generate. The influence of prayer on the human mind and body is as demonstrable as that of secreting glands. Its results can be measured in terms of increased physical buoyancy, greater intellectual vigour, moral stamina and a deeper understanding of the realities underlying human relationships.

If you make a habit of sincere prayer, your life will be very noticeably and profoundly altered. A tranquillity of bearing, a facial and bodily repose are observed in the lives of those whose inner lives are enriched. Within the depth of consciousness a flame kindles... thus begins a journey of the soul towards the realm of grace. *Prayer is a force as real as terrestrial gravity... it is the only power in the world that seems to overcome the laws of nature... a constant quieter miracle takes place hourly in the hearts of men and women who have discovered that prayer supplies them with a steady flow of sustaining power in their daily lives. Properly understood prayer is a mature activity indispensable to the fullest development of personality – the ultimate integration of man's highest faculties. Only in prayer do we achieve the complete and harmonious assembly of body, mind and spirit which gives the frail human reed its unshakable strength.*

Allexis Carrel

Live neither in the past (full of regret) nor in the future (worrying about what might be) but let each day absorb all your interest, energy and enthusiasm. The best preparation for tomorrow is to live today as fully as possible: do today's work superbly well.

Sir William Osler

Let there be many windows in your soul
that all the glory of the universe
may beautify it. Not the narrow pane
of one poor creed can catch the radiant rays
that shine from countless sources. Tear away
the blinds of superstition; let the light
pour through fair windows broad as truth itself
and high as Heaven.
Why should the spirit peer
through some priest-curtained orifice, and grope
along dim corridors of doubt, when all
the splendour from unfathomed seas of space
might bathe it with their golden seas of love?
Sweep up the debris of decaying faiths,
sweep down the cobwebs of worn-out beliefs,
and throw your soul wide open to the light
of reason and of knowledge. Tune your ear
to all the wordless music of the stars,
and to the voice of nature, and your heart
shall turn to truth and goodness, as the plant
turns to the sun. A thousand unseen hands
reach down to help you from their peace-crowned heights,
and all the forces of the firmament
shall fortify your strength. Be not afraid
to thrust aside half-truths and grasp the whole.

Ralph Waldo Trine
From *In Tune with the Infinite*

2nd Movement: Adagio tranquillo

2nd Movement: Adagio tranquillo

(slow / calm / quiet – when God seems silent)

Introduction to Second Movement

It is not always easy to see the way ahead – at times
when God seems silent – one can see a little perhaps – but
not far enough – as in a mist-laden wood – yet we know God IS there –
He has been there for us up to then – but where is He now? The trees
seem to block our way – the ground uncertain – the mist clouds the view
ahead – yet if we remain still – and wait –
instead of thrashing about in our doubt – our old certainties
will return as the mist clears.
As R.S.Thomas puts it so aptly in his classic "Kneeling" (pp. 106, 109)

"the meaning is in the waiting…"

and his "Folk Tale" (p. 110) reassuring us that we should continue in prayer
– even
when God seems silent – for

"Prayer is like gravel
flung at the sky's
window, hoping to attract
the loved one's
attention………………

I would
have refrained long since
but that peering once
through my locked fingers,
I thought I detected
the movement of a curtain."

Times of stillness and silence and solitude are tremendous opportunities
for spiritual growth – if only we would give ourselves up to it.
As P.D. James writes in *The Lighthouse* (p. 108)

"...the solitude had been a
revelation. He had never realised that to be completely alone
could be so satisfying and healing. "

I discover more and more each day my need for these times of solitude in which I can rediscover others with more truth and accept in the light of God my own weakness, ignorance, egoism and fear. This solitude does not separate me from others: it helps me love them more tenderly, realistically and attentively. I begin to distinguish between the false solitude which is a flight from others to be alone with egoism, sadness and a bruised sensitivity and true solitude which is a communion with God...

Jean Vanier
Community & Growth
From *The Fire of Silence and Stillness*

The recovery of the contemplative dimension of our lives, therefore, goes far beyond a change in behaviour. It is nothing less than a spiritual revolution that awakens deep levels of consciousness in us: not just the surface consciousness of our superficial self but the inner depth consciousness of our real self which we experience as nothing apart from the Being of God.

It is what the Fathers of the Church, especially the Eastern Fathers, like to call the discovery of the year: the heart, not as a physical organ, but as the centre of my being, the place where I am most truly myself, the place where I experience God...

William Shannon
Seeking the Face of God
From *The Fire of Silence and Stillness*
Edited by Paul Harris

O Spirit of God, set at rest the crowded, hurrying, anxious thoughts within our minds and hearts. Let the peace and quiet of thy presence take possession of us. Help us to rest, to relax, to become open and receptive to Thee. Thou dost know our inmost spirits, the hidden unconscious life within us, the forgotten memories of hurts and fears, the frustrated desires, the unresolved tensions and dilemmas. Cleanse and sweeten the springs of our being, that freedom, life and love may flow into both our conscious and hidden life.

Amen

George Appleton
From *A prayer for Quiet Hearts*
One Hundred Personal Prayers Old and New

Moments of great calm,
Kneeling before an altar
Of wood in a stone church
In summer, waiting for God
To speak; the air a staircase
For silence; the sun's light
Ringing me, as though I acted
A great role. And the audience
Still; all that close throng
Of spirits waiting, as I,
For the message.
Prompt me, God;
But not yet. When I speak,
Though it be you who speak
Through me, something is lost.
The meaning is in the waiting.

R.S.Thomas
From *Kneeling*

From this fair hill we see
The still, unsullied loveliness of Surrey;
Her heath and open downland,
Green meadows and fast-ripening corn,
Cool woods, and trees along her shaded lanes,
The hazel hedgerows of the countryside,
Her age-old trackways over the down,
Bold, rugged sandhills and clean, soaring pines,
Her bracken, ling and purple heather,
The blue of the shimmering summer heat
Where the sky and far-off Sussex meet,
And, on the turf at our feet
This flowering, wilding thyme
Whose fragrance on the wind
Is the sweet downland breath of Surrey

And, on the crest of the hill
An ageless church
Which, through wide-opened door,
Draws to its hallowed shrine
This downland beauty
Weaving it into so deep a joy
That through long years to come
We shall remember this fine hour
And, in remembering it
Be for a while
Lifted again above the stress
Of some drab passing day
Into this far lovelier realm
Of timeless peace and happiness.

John Sammes
St. Martha's, Pilgrim's Way

The solitude had been a revelation. He had never realised that to be completely alone could be so satisfying and healing. On his first visit he had wondered whether he would be able to endure it, but although the solitude compelled introspection, it was liberating rather than painful. He had returned to the traumas of his professional life changed in ways he couldn't explain....

P.D. James
From *The Lighthouse*

The air a staircase
For silence; the sun's light
Ringing me, as though I acted
A great role. And the audience
Still; all that close throng
Of spirits waiting as I
For the message.

Prompt me, God
But not yet. When I speak
Though it be you who speak
Through me, something is lost.
The meaning is in the waiting.

R.S.Thomas
From *Kneeling*

Prayer is like gravel
flung at the sky's
window, hoping to attract
the loved one's
attention. But without
visible plaits to let
down for the believer
to climb up,
to what purpose open
that far casement?
I would
have refrained long since
but that peering once
through my locked fingers,
I thought that I detected
the movement of a curtain.

R.S. Thomas
Folk Tale

There are many windows through which we can look out into the world, searching for meaning. There are those opened up by science, their panes polished by a succession of brilliant, penetrating minds. Through these we can see even further, even more clearly, into areas that once lay beyond human knowledge.

But there are other windows; windows that have been unshuttered by the logic of philosophers; windows through which the mystics seek their visions of the truth; windows from which the leaders of the great religions have peered as they search for purpose not only in the wondrous beauty of the world, but also in its darkness and ugliness. Most of us, when we ponder on the mystery of our existence, peer through but one of these windows onto the world. And even that one is often misted over by the breath of our finite humanity. We clear a tiny peephole and stare through. No wonder we are confused by the tiny fraction of a whole that we see. It is, after all, like trying to comprehend the panorama of the desert or sea through a rolled-up newspaper.

Jane Goodall
Through a Window

I have seen it standing up grey,
Gaunt, as though no sunlight
Could ever thaw out the music
Of its great bell; terrible
In its own way, for religion
Is like that. There are times
When a black frost is upon
One's whole being, and the heart
In its bone belfry hangs and is dumb.
But who is to know? Always,
Even in winter in the cold
Of a stone church, on his knees
Someone is praying, whose prayers fall
Steadily through the hard spell
Of weather that is between God
And himself. Perhaps it is the warm rain
That brings the sun and afterwards flowers,
On the raw graves and throbbing of bells.

R.S. Thomas
The Belfry

It is beautiful and still;
    the air rarefied
as the interior of a cathedral

expecting a presence. It is where also
    the harrier occurs,
materialising from nothing, snow

soft, but with claws of fire,
    quartering the bare earth
for the prey that escapes it;

hovering over the incipient
    scream, here a moment then
not here, like my belief in God.

R.S. Thomas
The Moorland

Often I try
To analyse the quality
Of its silences. Is this where God hides
From my searching? I have stopped to listen,
After the few people have gone,
To the air recomposing itself
For vigil. It has waited like this
Since the stones grouped themselves about it.
. . . . shadows advance
From their corners to take possession
Of places the light held
For an hour. The bats resume
Their business. The uneasiness of the pews
Ceases. There is no other sound
In the darkness but the sound of man
Breathing, testing his faith
Or emptiness, nailing his questions
One by one to an untenanted cross.

R.S. Thomas
In Church

"Quiet time alone, contemplation, prayer, music, a centering line of thought or reading, of study or work. It can be physical or intellectual or artistic, any creative life proceeding from oneself. It need not be an enormous project or a great work. But it should be something of one's own"... "What matters is that one be for a time inwardly attentive."

"Woman must be the pioneer in this turning inward for strength. In a sense she has always been the pioneer. Less able, until the last generation, to escape into outward activities, the very limitations of her life forced her to look inward. And from looking inward she gained an inner strength which man in his outward active life did not as often find"... "Men too, are being forced now to look inward – to find inner solutions as well as outer ones. Perhaps this change marks a new stage of maturity for modern extrovert, activist, materialistic Western man. Can it be that he is beginning to realize that the kingdom of heaven is within?"

"I cannot live for ever on my island but I can take the island shell back to my desk...to remind me that I must try to be alone for part of each year, even a week or a few days; and for part of each day, even for an hour or a few minutes in order to keep my core, my centre, my island-quality. Unless I keep the island-quality intact somewhere within me, I will have little to give my husband, my children, my friends or the world at large. The shell will remind me that woman must be still as the axis of a wheel in the midst of her activities; that she must be the pioneer in achieving this stillness, not only for her own salvation but for the salvation of family life, of society, perhaps even of our civilization."

Anne Morrow Lindbergh
From *Gift from the Sea*

When one is alone – these are among the most important times in one's life. Certain springs are tapped only when we are alone. The artist knows he must be alone to create; the writer, to work out his thoughts; the musician to compose; the saint, to pray. But women need solitude in order to find again the true essence of themselves: that firm strand which will be the indispensable centre of a whole web of human relationships. She must find that inner stillness which has been described by Charles Morgan as "the stilling of the soul within the activities of the mind and body so that it might be still as the axis of a revolving wheel is still."

The beautiful image is to my mind the one that women could hold before their eyes. This is an end toward which we could strive – to be the still axis within the revolving wheel of relationships, obligations and activities. Solitude alone is not the answer to this; it is only a step toward it, a mechanical aid, like the "room of one's own" demanded for women, before they could make their place in the world. The problem is not entirely in finding the room of one's own, the time alone, difficult and necessary as this is. The problem is more how to still the soul in the midst of its activities. In fact, the problem is how to feed the soul.

Anne Morrow Lindbergh
From *Gift from the Sea*

In today's world silence is in short supply; this is a serious problem for our society, and anything we can do to help people recover a sense of silence as a necessary and positive element in human life is a contribution to the general sanity. Many people can, however, contrive some islands of silence in their lives, perhaps in holiday time. Without romantically ignoring our dependence on our environment it is also true to say that silence is partly an interior quality; you can learn to live from your own deep centre, rather than in the ego with its clamorous demands. You can make positive use of any period of silence that does occur, rather than looking on it as an empty stretch of time to be endured or filled up somehow. Silence like this is not a threat to us but an invitation to depth, to listening, to a loving communion in joy.

Maria Boulding
From *The Coming of God*

Music can...introduce us to a 'meantime' where there is an acute sense of delay but which is at the same time enormously enriching.

Music does this most powerfully through silence. All composers and musicians know that silence is one of the most effective tools they have. The opening of the theme music of the film *Jaws* generates its 'edge-of-the-seat' terror largely through silence.   The final bars of Sibelius' Fifth symphony are, in essence, silence punctuated by six chords, creating an extraordinarily intense longing for resolution. In this example, the silences become highly charged because of the memory of what has been and the anticipation of what will be; so we are 'pulled' more profoundly into the music's drama.

One of the hardest aspects of the Christian life is handling the silences of God, the apparently dead 'in between' times. Music can remind us of the power of memory and anticipation – the memory of what God has done in Jesus Christ, and in that, the promise of what he will finally do for the world. This can draw us back into God's ways with the world, and thus renew our trust and hope. Something of this dynamic, surely, needs to find its way into at least some forms of silent prayer. Music does more than help us understand the dynamic. It enacts it for us, it offers the experience of a potentially empty silence becoming full, vibrant and charged with hope.

Jeremy Begbie
Prayer and Music
From *Perspectives on Prayer*, edited by Fraser Watts

Be very still before this beauty
That nothing asks of you.
Let not the wind of thought arise
Or the sunlight of your worship
Make no track upon it with eager footsteps.
Be very still before this beauty.
Offering in silence the landscape of your heart
To the falling of the snow.

Clare Cameron
The White Snow of Meditation
From: *The Bridge is Love*
An anthology of hope collected by
Elizabeth Basset

...There is a pool of tranquillity within each one of us, a centre of silence and peace. There the whole being may be renewed. There the strength of the Father may be felt. To sit beside this pool at least once each day is to replenish and rejuvenate our being.

Without this period of silence and contemplation our whole life starts to disintegrate into chaos, frustration and despair. We have then cut ourselves off from our source and from our purpose.

The more often we can find a moment or two to sit beside our pool of stillness, the greater will be our strength for then our strength is the strength of the Father as he works His Will through us and we will dwell in the house of the Lord for ever.

Henry Thomas Hamblin
The Science of Thought Review
From *The Bridge is Love*
An anthology of hope collected by
Elizabeth Basset

[The early Friends] made the discovery that silence is one of the best preparations for communion [with God] and for the reception of inspiration and guidance. Silence itself, of course has no magic. It may be just sheer emptiness, absence of words or noise or music. It may be an occasion for slumber, or it may be a dead form. But it may be an intensified pause, a vitalised hush, a creative quiet, an actual moment of mutual and reciprocal correspondence with God.

The actual meeting of man with God and God with man is the very crown and culmination of what we do with our human life here on earth.

Rufus M.Jones
From *Christian Faith and Practice in the Experience of the Religious Society of Friends*

3rd Movement: Tempestosa

(stormy / fast – when life is tough / problematic)

Introduction to Third Movement

This Movement brings us to the most challenging aspects of our faith
when storm clouds threaten to overwhelm us and
life presents insurmountable problems.
Where is God now – when we need Him most?

Still there – for

"God does not die on the day when we cease to believe in a personal
deity but we
die on the day when our lives cease to be illumined by the steady
radiance, renewed daily, of a wonder – the source of which is beyond all
reason"

so writes Dag Hammarskjold (p. 129)

and again Arnold Toynbee (p. 132) –

"A human being may believe sincerely that he has no religion but in
moments of crisis his religion will assert itself.
When he is confronted with his own imminent death
or when he is afflicted with bereavement, disappointment, self-reproach or
any other form of acute spiritual suffering, he will find himself living, even if
only for a moment
on the spiritual plane which he has tried to dismiss as illusion. I therefore
feel certain that there is a future for religious belief."

And as the music of this Third Movement builds and builds into a reassuring
climax, we are stirred further by Clifford Bax's great piece (p. 138) urging
Man to

"Turn back O Man, forswear thy foolish ways..."

For many of man's troubles are self-inflicted:

"Ours is not a chaotic universe but a universe of laws and they include moral
laws. We ignore them individually at the risk
of our immortal souls and mankind ignores them collectively
at the risk of its... existence."

Sobering words from Paul Johnson (p. 139)

I stand between the years. The Light of My Presence is flung across the year to come – the radiance of the Sun of Righteousness. Backward, over the past year, is My Shadow thrown, hiding trouble and sorrow and disappointment.

Dwell not on the past – only on the present. Only use the past as the trees use My Sunlight to absorb it, to make from it in after days the warming fire-rays. So store only the blessings from Me, the Light of the World. Encourage yourselves by the thought of these.

Bury every fear of the future, of poverty for those dear to you, of suffering, of loss. Bury all thought of unkindness and bitterness, all your dislikes, your resentments, your sense of failure, your disappointment in others and in yourselves, your gloom, your despondency, and let us leave them all, buried and go forward to a new and risen life.

Remember that you must not see as the world sees. I hold the year in My Hands – in trust for you. But I shall guide you one day at a time.

Leave the rest with Me. You must not anticipate the gift by fears or thoughts of the days ahead.

And for each day I shall supply the wisdom and the strength.

Between the Years
From *God Calling by Two Listeners*

All our peace, while we are in this mortal life, rests more in the humble endurance of troubles and of things that are irksome to us than in not feeling them at all. For no man is here without some trouble. Therefore, he who can suffer best will have most peace, and he who is the true conqueror of himself is the true lord of the world, the friend of Christ and the true inheritor of the kingdom of heaven.

Thomas à Kempis
The Imitation of Christ

God does not die on the day when we cease to believe in a personal deity, but we die on the day when our lives cease to be illumined by the steady radiance, renewed daily, of a wonder, the source of which is beyond all reason.

Dag Hammarskjold
Markings

Life affords no higher pleasure than that of surmounting difficulties, passing from one step of success to another, forming new wishes, and seeing them gratified. He that labours in any great or laudable undertaking has his fatigues first supported by hope and afterwards rewarded by joy...

To strive with difficulties, and to conquer them, is the highest human felicity.

Samuel Johnson

Do not look forward to the changes and chances of this life in fear; rather look to them with hope that, as they arise, God, whose you are, will deliver you out of them. He has kept you hitherto – do you but hold fast to his dear hand and he will lead you safely through all things; and when you cannot stand, he will bear you in his arms.

St. Francis de Sales

A human being may believe sincerely that he has no religion but in moments of crisis his religion will assert itself. When he is confronted with his own imminent death, or when he is afflicted with bereavement, disappointment, self-reproach or any other form of acute spiritual suffering, he will find himself living, even if only for a moment, on the spiritual plane which he has tried to dismiss as illusion. I therefore feel certain that there is a future for religious belief.

Arnold Toynbee
Article in *The Listener*

The theologians who responded to the Holocaust had to abandon many of the ideas about God they had previously held. Like Darwin, they were unable to believe in an omnipotent God who was also beneficent, all loving. If God existed, God could no longer be both loving and omnipotent: if God was omnipotent, then God clearly was not loving; if God was loving then God could not be omnipotent. The only God who could retain our allegiance was a suffering God. It is, of course, easier to abandon God than to go on making excuses for him. Yet many of us cannot quite do that.

There is something about life itself that calls us to believe, even though our faith co-exists with pain and doubt. We believe that life is more than sorrow and horror. There is also beauty and meaning; there is love and compassion; there are great saints and great souls. All of these pose as much of a problem as evil: how did they arise in a meaningless universe? The answer of faith is that some purpose of love lies behind it all. We cannot prove its existence; indeed there are times when we hold on to the belief in spite of what appears to be overwhelming evidence against it. Yet it continues to assert itself against all meaninglessness, against the view of the universe as a pitiless accident. At our most beleaguered we choose to go on believing as an act of defiance against the great emptiness that threatens to engulf us. If the universe is ultimately pitiless and without meaning, then we are better than all of it because we are also capable of compassion; we are able to cry at the sorrow of it and be moved with love for the beauty of it; and these are greater things than emptiness, they are more powerful than the great void. So we go on saying *yes*, trusting that our confidence, however frail, is responding to some great love beyond ourselves that haunts the universe.

Richard Holloway
Why Does God Allow Suffering?
From *Dancing on the Edge*

The modern world notably lacks images of splendour, having come to settle for merely human priorities.

It is difficult to imagine the intimations of the divine presence; there are no longer splendid courts or exulted rulers whose style simulated on earth projections of supreme authority.   Our human accomplishments, often these days falsely described as "spiritual values" – like art and music – are a mean substitute for the presence of God.   Our daily lives, bereft of religious references of the sort which in traditional societies marked the passage of time, are preoccupied with apparent urgencies which, like the thorns in the Parable of the Sower, exclude authentic spiritual formation.

Edward Norman
A Meditation
From: *Raised to Glory*

We shall have to repent in this generation, not so much for the evil deeds of the wicked people, but for the appalling silence of the good.

Martin Luther King

God has created me to do Him some definite service; He has committed some work to me which He has not committed to another. I have my mission – I may never know it in this life, but I shall be told it in the next.

I am a link in a chain, a bond of connection between persons. He has not created me for naught. I shall do good, I shall do His work. I shall be an angel of peace, a preacher of truth in my own place *while not intending it* – if I do but keep his Commandments.

Therefore I will trust Him. Whatever, wherever I am, I can never be thrown away. If I am in sickness, my sickness may serve Him; in perplexity, my perplexity may serve Him; if I am in sorrow, my sorrow may serve Him. He does nothing in vain. He knows what He is about. He may take away my friends, He may throw me among strangers. He may make me feel desolate, make my spirit sink, hide my future from me – still He knows what He is about.

Cardinal Newman
Meditation

Summer devours us with distractions,
As near as the shrub-rose at the door,
The hub-hub in the hall.

But when the wounded sun lies in the earth,
And snow is being unskeined from the sky
In fold after fold,
There is time to contemplate the winter
In solitudes of snow,
In the necessary distance of the human voice,
In the silence of the empty hall.

Wanting solitude so long, strange to find silence
Itself so noisy with sound. Does the ear seek
The wind's complaint under the door,
The little draught playing in the chandelier?
Is it fear that twitches and writhes
In the shadows, furnishes
The dark corner of the hall with threats?

And afterwards there's the inner debate.
Silence made loud with interminable discourse,
Nowhere to escape the trivial chattering,
No landscape inviolate from the tip
Of one's own smouldering rubbish.

Perhaps only the privileged find it.
The mystic's void scraped clear to a flawless
Perfection. Or the tortured few
In their suffering's grossest extremity
Find they're no longer alone.

Heather Buck
Distractions

Turn back O Man, forswear thy foolish ways.
Old now is Earth, and none may count her days,
Yet thou, her child, whose head is crowned with flame,
Still wilt not hear thine inner God proclaim
"Turn back O Man, forswear thy foolish ways."
Earth might be fair and all men glad and wise,
Age after age their tragic empires rise.
Built while they dream and in that dreaming weep.
Would man but wake from out his haunted sleep
Earth shall be fair, and all her people one,
Nor till that hour shall God's whole will be done.
Now, even now, once more from earth to sky
Peals forth in joy man's old undaunted cry
"Earth shall be fair, and all her folk be one."

Clifford Bax
Music by Gustav Holst (1874-1934)

Ours is not a chaotic universe but a universe of laws, and they include moral laws. We ignore them individually at the risk of our immortal souls, and mankind ignores them collectively at the risk of its social health and even its existence.

Paul Johnson
From *Our Quest for God*

There was a great piled up mass of clouds with the sun setting behind them; a fighting sunset, but so grand, and I sat and wondered and wondered what *was* the meaning of things, and what is the meaning of us, tiny people with our huge faith – because it is a huge faith to believe what we believe. We're such scraps over against a sunset like that, that it doesn't *seem* as if it could matter what we are, or much what we did; and yet it matters so enormously. Why? It would be lovely *not* to matter and yet hateful, and everything is like that. The ache of God in you and the weariness of your denial of it – all bewildering and contradictory.

J. H. Oldham
From *Florence Allshorn and The Story of St.Julian's*

Does the road wind up hill all the way?
    Yes, to the very end.
Will the day's journey take the whole long day?
    From morn to night, my friend.

But is there for the night a resting place?
    A roof for when the slow, dark hours begin.
May not the darkness hide it from my face?
    You cannot miss that inn.

Shall I meet other wayfarers at night?
    Those who have gone before.
Then must I knock or call when just in sight?
    They will not keep you waiting at that door.

Shall I find comfort, travel-sore and weak?
    Of labour you shall find the sum.
Will there be beds for me and all who seek?
    Yes, beds for all who come.

Christina Rossetti (1830-1894)
Uphill

But we must not disguise from ourselves that God's dealings with this world are still a very difficult problem... It is useless to say "God's in His heaven; All's right with the world," when many things are obviously all wrong in the world. It is vain to argue...that divine justice is an automatic self-adjusting machine, so that all get their deserts (not of course in a grossly material sense) in this life. Eminent literary men in the last century were too secure and comfortable to see what a rough place the world is for the majority of those who live in it. It was only after long travail of soul that the Jews learned their lesson; we shall not learn ours by turning epigrams. Remember that complacent optimism, no less than pessimism, is treason against Hope. The world, as it is, is not good enough to be true. We ought not to be satisfied with it. "God has prepared some better thing..." ...

This world exists for the realization in time of God's eternal purposes. Some of these are bound up with individual lives, for God intended each one of us to do and to be something; others have a far wider scope, and require far more time for their fulfilment. The manifold evils in the world are allowed to exist because only through them can the greater good be brought into activity. This greater good is not any external achievement, but the love and heroism and self-sacrifice which the great conflict calls into play...

W.R. Inge

It is not enough to teach techniques. We want to develop young people for a wholesome and hopeful generation – for a generation which believes in the value of the humanities, which will face the problems of our time honestly and without fear, with the deep will to understand other men and to learn to build a better future.

Technique alone, without any moral and ethical point of departure or aim, has brought us to the very edge of a universal catastrophe that we have in no way overcome. To achieve this necessary future victory over ourselves and the terrifying world that we have created, we will need to find again a synthesis between technical knowledge and spiritual content. ... It is thus for every one of us – to help build towards a more human way of life, one that can lead man in the coming generations to personal dignity, integrity and peace.

If we want the life of man as a whole to have a deeper content, with a cultural basis, we must educate every single human being to find a deeper spiritual content for his own life.

We must develop, cultivate, inspire and discipline the creative and spiritual abilities of man. We must not waste, corrupt or slant for material purposes those qualities that make him more than an animal: his sense of beauty, his idea of truth, his ability to think, his creative intuition and his vision of God.

We know that there are many men and women... people who are searching for more than they are finding.

We have solved many technical difficulties and most of the restrictions of materials and machines; but we have lost in the process of an increasingly materialistic education, the essential relation to nature, to man and to God.

Marguerite Wildenhain
Pottery, Form and Expression
The Virago Book of Spirituality

Strange as it may seem, evil exists to further man's development... if man is to be free then *he* must be able to choose between good and evil... If man allows himself to be led astray and difficulties or catastrophes are the result, there is little point in accusing the Deity of neglect.   Man, collectively, is responsible.   At best he might, like Solomon, ask God for wisdom but what is not learnt through wisdom will be learnt by experience and this may be hard.

What must be realized is that evil and freedom arise from the same source. The evolution of evil is permitted for the sake of human freedom...   The question arises as to whether man can use his freedom in a positive way or whether he will succumb to the blandishments of his tempters.

The biblical story of Job makes illustrative reading. God allows Satan to afflict Job in many ways but Job remains steadfast throughout. Finally he demands to know the reason for his suffering i.e. through the questions arising in his soul, his thinking force is awakened.   In the end he is spiritually as well as materially, richer than before.

As physical strength grows by contending with physical objects, so moral strength grows by contending with adversity. Thus evil has a purpose in the divine plan...

Roy Wilkinson
From *Rudolf Steiner*
An introduction to his spiritual world-view.

Hill, sea and sky
meeting in a ribbon sparkle;
A breeze speaks for God,
tunnels of green with eyelet glimpses of a
meadow beyond;
Eight Bells bidding welcome;
churches tucked in a jewelled crown –
crowning our God;
Finding the clatter of chatter like
beans in an empty tin –
Longing for minds
that meet the passion of other links
long gone;
And whence now?
Waiting on God –
Fierce to speak;
Growing impatient with those who cannot,
will not see as she;
Blocking the clarion call to look deeper;
The churches – open – waiting for souls to come
shunning mortal pleasure
seeking the deeper, more lasting jewel,
seeing with a reaching eye.
No crunch of feet on gravel –
their feet do not find the way:
too busy with their filled days –
no curiosity there.
So man continues
not to heed the word
And the prophet goes silently beside them –
Unheard.

Anna Jeffery
From *A Sussex Dream*
Alfriston – October 2006

"Do you think that evil is a positive force at large in the world?"

"I think evil is a positive force at large in all of us. I've always believed that the battle that rages inside us is just a miniature of the battle that rages in the world in general. I think that within us we all carry the seeds of our destruction and of our own salvation."

David Puttnam
in conversation with Joan Bakewell
in the BBC Radio 3 series: *Belief*

...this black figure knelt at the centre of reality and force and with the movements of her will and lips controlled spiritual destinies for eternity. There ran out from this peaceful chapel lines of spiritual power that lost themselves in the distance, bewildering in their profusion and terrible in the intensity of their hidden power.

F.C. Happold
The Journey Inwards
From *Love is My Meaning*
An anthology of Assurance collected by
Elizabeth Basset

If I should stoop
Into a dark tremendous sea of cloud,
It is but for a time; I press God's lamp
Close to my breast; its splendour soon or late
Will pierce the gloom; I shall emerge one day

Robert Browning
Parting at Morning
From *Love is My Meaning*
An anthology of assurance collected by
Elizabeth Basset

We are not here to curse the darkness, but to light the candle that can guide us through that darkness to a safe and sane future

John F. Kennedy

It is not by regretting what is irreparable that true work is to be done but by making the best use of what we are. It is not by complaining that we have not the right tools but by using well the tools we have. What we are and where we are is God's providential arrangement and God's doing though it may be man's misdoing – and the manly and the wise way is to look your disadvantages in the face and see what can be made of them.

Frederick Robertson

God does not cause our misfortunes. Some are caused by bad luck, some are caused by bad people, and some are simply an inevitable consequence of our being human and being moral, living in a world of inflexible natural laws.

The painful things that happen to us are not punishments for our misbehaviour, nor are they in any way part of some grand design on God's part.

Because the tragedy is not God's will, we need not feel hurt or betrayed by God when tragedy strikes.

We can turn to Him for help in overcoming it, precisely because we can tell ourselves that God is as outraged by it as we are.

Harold S. Kushner

Jan Walgrave once commented that our age constitutes a virtual conspiracy against the interior life. What he meant is not that there is somewhere a conscious conspiracy against proper values, the churches and true spirituality, as paranoid conservatism likes to believe. What he meant was that, today, a number of historical circumstances are blindly flowing together and accidentally conspiring to produce a climate within which it is difficult not just to think about God or to pray, but simply to have any interior depth whatsoever. The air we breathe today is generally not conducive to interiority and depth.

Why? What factors are accidentally conspiring to cause this? ... Among the many things that work against interiority today, three can be singled out as particularly cankerous: *narcissism, pragmatism, and unbridled restlessness.*

Narcissism means excessive self-preoccupation; pragmatism means excessive focus on work, achievement and the practical concerns of life; and restlessness means an excessive greed for experience – an over-eating – not in terms of food but in terms of trying to drink in too much of life. Narcissism accounts for our heartaches, pragmatism for our headaches and restlessness for our insomnia. And the combination of all three together account for the fact that we are so habitually self-absorbed by heartaches, headaches and greed for experience that we rarely find the time and space to be in touch with the deeper movements inside of and around us.

There is no limit to rich analysis on this: Thomas Merton once said that the biggest spiritual problem of our time is efficiency, work, pragmatism; by the time we keep the plant running there is little time and energy for anything else. Neil Postman suggests that, as a culture, we are amusing ourselves to death, that is, distracting ourselves into a bland, witless superficiality. Henri Nouwen has written eloquently on how our greed for experience and the restlessness, hostility and fantasy it generates blocks solitude, hospitality and prayer in our lives. They are right. What each of these authors and countless others, are saying is that we, for every kind of reason, good and bad, are distracting ourselves into spiritual oblivion.

Ronald Rolheiser
Chapter II: The Current Struggles with Christian Spirituality
From **Seeking Spirituality**

We want to be saints but we also want to feel every sensation experienced by sinners; we want to be innocent and pure, but we also want to be experienced and taste all of life; we want to serve the poor and have a simple lifestyle but we also want all the comforts of the rich; we want to have the depth afforded by solitude, but we also do not want to miss anything; we want to pray, but we also want to watch television, read, talk to friends and go out. Small wonder life is often a trying enterprise and we are often tired and pathologically over-extended.

Medieval philosophy had a dictum that said: every choice is a renunciation. Indeed. Every choice is a thousand renunciations. To choose one thing is to turn one's back on many others. To marry one person is to not marry all the others, to have a baby means to give up certain other things; and to pray is to miss watching television or visiting friends. This makes choosing hard. No wonder we struggle so much with commitment. It is not that we do not want certain things, it is just that we know that if we choose them we close off so many other things. It is not easy to be a saint, to will the one thing, to have the discipline of a Mother Teresa.

Ronald Rolheiser
What is Spirituality?
From *Seeking Spirituality*

[Faith is] a sense of joy and confidence, a sense that you can exist amidst the suffering and pain of life with serenity and confidence. It is not that you don't feel it – religion is not an anaesthetic – but it means you will feel able to deal with it.

Extract from an interview with Karen Armstrong
Conversations on Religion
Edited by Mick Gordon and Chris Wilkinson

4th Movement: Finale

(end of life / journey's end / into harbour)

Introduction to Fourth Movement

Here – as in the radiant sky of life's sunset,
this Symphony of Life climaxes with a Finale summed up by
Rudyard Kipling's "When Earth's Last Picture is Painted" (p. 162)

And George Eliot's masterpiece: "O may I join the choir invisible..." (p. 163)

Not forgetting T.S.Eliot: "We shall not cease from exploration..." (p. 172)

And finally – the Venerable Bede – comparing life with the flight of a lone
sparrow through a banqueting hall...(p. 173)

All these voices – all these notes – in this movement, represent the time we
all have to face, sooner or later, when our life here draws to a close:

"...the mighty symphony which fills the universe
to which our lives are destined to make their tiny contribution and which is
the self-expression of the Eternal God."

So writes Evelyn Underhill in her classic piece: *The Spiritual Life*

I said to the man
Who stood at the gate of the year
"Give me a light that I may tread safely
into the unknown."
And he replied,
"Go into the darkness
and put your hand into the hand of God
That shall be to you
better than light
and safer than a known way!"
So I went forth
And finding the Hand of God
Trod gladly into the night.
He led me towards the hills
And the breaking of day in the lone east.
So heart be still!
What need our human life to know
If God hath comprehension?
In all the dizzy strife of things,
Both high and low,
God hideth his intention.

M. Louise Haskins
From *I said to the man*

"How did you get to be so strong?"

"I was at peace with myself, that's all."

"Well then, how did you get to be at peace with yourself?"

"By accepting that things change, that they will and must change. It's the natural order of things. All the time you are growing, developing, changing, everyone and everything around you is doing the same."

Judith Miller
From *Blythe Spirit*

When Earth's last picture is painted and the tubes are
 twisted and dried,
When the oldest colours have faded, and the youngest
 critic has died,
We shall rest, and, faith, we shall need it – lie down for an
 aeon or two,
Till the Master of All Good Workmen shall put us to work
 anew.

And those that were good shall be happy: they shall sit in
 a golden chair;
They shall splash at a ten-league canvas with brushes of
 comet's hair.
They shall find real saints to draw from – Magdalene,
 Peter and Paul;
They shall work for an age at a sitting and never be tired
 at all!

And only The Master shall praise us, and only The Master
 shall blame;
And no one shall work for money, and no one shall work
 for fame,
But each for the joy of the working, and each, in his
 separate star,
Shall draw the Thing as he sees it for the God of Things as
 They are!

Rudyard Kipling
From *When Earth's Last Picture is Painted*

O may I join the choir invisible
Of those immortal dead who live again
In minds made better by their presence; live
In pulses stirred to generosity,
In deeds of daring rectitude, in scorn
Of miserable aims that end with self,
In thoughts sublime that pierce the night like stars,
And with their mild persistence urge men's minds
To vaster issues...
    May I reach
That purest heaven – be to other souls
The cup of strength in some great agony,
Enkindle generous ardour, feed pure love,
Beget the smiles that have no cruelty,
Be the sweet presence of good diffused,
And in diffusion ever more intense!
So shall I join the choir invisible,
Whose music is the gladness of the world.

George Eliot

When you leave this world, material riches will be left behind; but every good that you have done will go with you.

Life should be chiefly service. Without that ideal, the intelligence that God has given you is not reaching out toward its goal. When in service, you forget the little self, you will feel the big Self of Spirit

Paramahansa Yogananda

I see them working in old rectories
By the sun's light, by candlelight,
Venerable men, their black cloth
A little dusty, a little green
With holy mildew. And yet their skulls,
Ripening over so many prayers,
Toppled into the same grave
With oafs and yokels. They left no books,
Memorial to their lonely thought
In grey parishes; rather they wrote
On men's hearts and in the minds
Of young children. Sublime words
Too soon forgotten. God in his time
Or out of time, will correct this.

R.S. Thomas
The Country Clergy

"In the evening, after the day trippers have gone, a deep tranquillity settles over the village. One by one, lights come on in the cottages, residents stroll about in the gentle air, and a sense of enchantment is everywhere."
Australian Gourmet

"That night, when we reached our suite, its wide windows revealed a scene of ephemeral splendour. The sea's silent invasion of the estuary was complete. The tide had flooded the sand. A full moon silvered the water. Beyond, dark mounded hills bore clusters of lights like earthbound stars."
The Washington Post

Portmeirion Reviewed
From a brochure some years following the fire in June 1981

Bereavement is a complex thing. One cannot deal with it simply by assuring the stricken person that all is well with his loved one. Intellectually, he may be well aware of that fact. Belief in a benevolent, glowing new opportunity in the life beyond could be one of the very cornerstones of a person's character, and yet that person could experience a seemingly unendurable grief. One must separate out the other elements of the agony of bereavement before the clear knowledge of the re-energising nature of the new life can do its healing, restorative work.

Life, as actually lived by us, is very largely a matter of emotional relationships – tugs and pulls, attractions and repulsions – between human beings. In this sense, each of our lives is made up of the lives of others. When one life is seemingly removed from this earth plane, the whole pattern shakes and those closest to the one who has 'graduated' *(to the next world)* are most deeply affected. Ties with cosmic and spiritual life and its greater perspectives can ease this pain but not eliminate it. On the earth plane our spiritual bodies are incubating and our earth bodies have a powerful sway. They have their habits, their appetites, their imprints, their long conditioning in familiar ways. When one of these behaviour circuits must be drastically rearranged, the result is unavoidable pain.

When this disruption is severe, it may stir up a whole nest of deeply buried feelings that the bereaved is now forced to contend with. These feelings are so common and so widespread – as well as so intense – that they were among the subjects to which Sigmund Freud gave his pioneering attention. Beside the simple sadness because of loss, Freud sometimes found a complicated network of dejection, loss of interest in real experience and feelings of being punished or expecting to be punished. He pointed out that just because a person was physically gone did not mean that the person's imprint, deepened perhaps over years, was not still vivid in the mourner's memory. The tension between absence and emotional presence needs to be recognised. "The normal outcome," wrote Freud, "is that deference for reality gains the day." The realities of course, are spiritual ones. A healthy mind, aided by the understanding and solicitude of friends, gradually finds that earth impressions fade as the truth of the ever-opening continuance of human life takes over. Sometimes, says Freud, it is slow. "Each single one of the memories and hopes which bound the libido to the object is brought up... and detachment...is accomplished." Though the process may be slow, it is, given faith, sure.

Arthur Ford
The Life Beyond Death

Dying? ... I almost did it once before and found it one of the great, memorable, ecstatic experiences of my life. I can see no reason why the real thing should be less joyous than the trial run. I know that great opportunities await us where we are all going. I hope, when the time comes, I will have completed that earth task for which I believe my life in the earth sphere was fashioned: to use whatever special talents were given me, through no merit of mine, to remove for all time the fear of the death passage from earth minds, and to raise the curtain a little bit for a glimpse of the glory beyond.

Arthur Ford
The Life Beyond Death

I have one last thing to say. The world appears to be taking a path which is slowly leading it nearer to catastrophe. You and I know this with our minds although we dare not let ourselves *feel* it too much. I send this little book out into the world at such a time as this, in the hope that it will bear with it some encouragement to meet these days with serenity. In spite of many prophets of doom, I do not believe there is anything determined or inevitable in the world situation which justifies despair. The forces of evil working on both sides, have always used fear as one of their most effective weapons, and they are at work visibly and audibly at the present time. Let us not forget that there are also spiritual powers at work in the world for good, and that they work for the large part silently and without ostentation. We can offer our greatest help to them by our state of mind. We can refuse to be afraid. We can refuse to be caught up in any collective emotion of hate or antagonism for those who are regarded as potential enemies. We can constantly pray for those in the world who are disinterestedly working for peace. We can practise in our personal life those attitudes of goodwill to difficult neighbours which are so much needed on the national level. Life and Death are not issues which are wholly within our power to determine either as to time or circumstance. It is only asked of us that both on familiar paths and in the crises of change, we are worthy habitations of an immortal spirit.

> You that have faith to look with fearless eyes
> Beyond the tragedy of a world at strife,
> And trust that out of night and death shall rise
> The dawn of ampler life:
>
> Rejoice, whatever anguish rend your heart
> That God has given you, for a priceless dower,
> To live in these great times and have your part
> In Freedom's crowning hour.

That you may tell your sons who see the light
  High in the heavens their heritage to take:
"I saw the powers of darkness put to flight!
   I saw the morning beak!"

Raynor C. Johnson
From: *Final Reflections, A Religious Outlook for Modern Man*

We shall not cease from exploration
And the end of all our exploring
Will be to arrive where we started
And know the place for the first time.
Through the unknown, remembered gate
When the last of earth left to discover
Is that which was the beginning;
At the source of the longest river
The voice of the hidden waterfall
And the children in the apple-tree
Not known, because not looked for
But heard, half-heard in the stillness
Between two waves of the sea.
Quick now, here, now, always –
A condition of complete simplicity
(Costing not less than everything)
And all shall be well and
All manner of things shall be well
When the tongues of flame are in-folded
Into the crowned knot of fire
And the fire and the rose are one.

T.S. Eliot
From *Four Quartets*

'Your Majesty, when we compare the present life of man with that time of which we have no knowledge, it seems to me like the swift flight of a lone sparrow through the banqueting-hall where you sit in the winter months to dine with your thanes and counsellors. Inside there is a comforting fire to warm the room; outside the wintry storms of snow and rain are raging. This sparrow flies swiftly in through one door of the hall, and out through another. While he is inside, he is safe from the winter storms; but after a few moments of comfort, he vanishes from sight into the darkness whence he came. Similarly, man appears on earth for a little while, but we know nothing of what went before this life, and what follows. Therefore if this new teaching can reveal any more certain knowledge, it seems only right that we should follow it.'

The Venerable Bede
From *A History of the English Church and People*

When we come to the end...believing that He...will be able to take what we have done for Him, whether explicitly or implicitly, He will gather it into His Kingdom, to be in that Kingdom as that particular enrichment of the Kingdom's glory which our particular life has to contribute.

For there is something which only you can bring into the Kingdom.

Eric Abbott
Dean of Westminster
From *The Compassion of God and the Passion of Christ*

We do not live in a purely functional universe, thank God, but rather in a miraculous convergence of mysterious activities which insist, if we are truly open-minded, that even the most down-to-earth facts and phenomena point to the transcendent, inviting our wonder and worship.

Michael Marshall
From *Church of England Newspaper*
September 2003

Don't let me die in the dark, Lord
And not on a winter's day
And not in the afternoon, Lord
When the light is slipping away

But let me go in the morning, Lord
In the sunshine, in the spring
So it won't seem so much like the end, Lord
But the start of everything

A Prayer

....at death ...shall we see all our past at once? Is death the passage from the successive to the simultaneous – that is, from time to eternity? Shall we then understand, in its unity, the poem or mysterious episode of our existence, which till then we have spelled out phrase by phrase? And is this the secret of that glory which so often enwraps the brow and countenance of those who are newly dead? If so, death would be like the arrival of a traveller at the top of a great mountain, whence he sees spread out before him the whole configuration of the country, of which till then he had had but passing glimpses. To be able to overlook one's own history, to divine its meaning in the general concert and in the divine plan, would be the beginning of eternal felicity. Till then we had sacrificed ourselves to the universal order, but then we should understand and appreciate the beauty of that order. **We had toiled and laboured under the conductor of the orchestra; and we should find ourselves become surprised and delighted hearers.** We had seen nothing but our own little path in the mist; and suddenly a marvellous panorama and boundless distances would open before our dazzled eyes...

Henri-Frederic Amiel
From *A Diary of Readings* by John Baillie

...we must never forget the tremendous value and importance of our earth lives. We learn lessons here that can be learned nowhere else; and, after some trial and much error, I have realized that it is a great mistake to concentrate on the 'hereafter' at the expense of here. We are all harnessed, or should be, to the needs of the age.

Our impediment, very difficult to shift, is that 'only religious people believe this sort of stuff.' I think that if it could be grasped that we don't become bodiless wraiths, ghosts, shades or spirits when we die, but develop and inhabit a body if you like of finer matter, a subtle body, an etheric body – if this were grasped as true for all of us, whether or no we ever go to church, and true for all living things, sceptics might perhaps be less unwilling to suspend disbelief. Sensitives can see 'the dead' in their new bodies. I think it is possible that within the next (say) hundred years many more people will. Ordinary people like myself see and hear in flashes; and of course certain animals are much more finely equipped than humans with extended vision and hearing. ...

...the mystical life can never be susceptible to the kind of proof that some (doubters) require. Only direct experience can convince a doubter, once and for all: convince the doubter, that is, – not anybody else! Still I have had the immense happiness of helping to convince several bereaved friends during these last years; or rather, I have been able to put them in the way of finding their own certainty.

Rosamond Lehmann
From *The Swan in the Evening*

This is my idea of immortality. An endless life of helpful change, with the instinct, the longing to rise, to learn, to love, to get nearer the source of all good, and go on from the lowest plane to the highest, rejoicing more and more as we climb into the clearer light, the purer air, the happier life which must exist, for, as Plato said, "The soul cannot imagine what does not exist because it is the shadow of God who knows and creates all things."

Louisa May Alcott
From *The Selected Letters*

The spiritual life, then, is not a peculiar or extreme form of piety. It is, on the contrary, that full and real life for which man is made; a life that is organic and social, essentially free, yet with its own necessities and laws. Just as physical life means, and depends on, constant correspondence with our physical environment, the atmosphere that surrounds and penetrates us, the energies of heat and light, whether we happen to notice it or not; so does spiritual life mean constant correspondence with our spiritual environment, whether we notice it or not. We get out of gear in either department, when this correspondence is arrested or disturbed; and if it stops altogether, we cease to live. For the most part, of course, the presence and action of the great spiritual universe surrounding us is no more noticed by us than the pressure of air on our bodies, or the action of light. Our field of attention is not wide enough for that; our spiritual senses are not sufficiently alert.

Most people work so hard developing their correspondence with the visible world, that their power of corresponding with the invisible is left in a rudimentary state. But when, for one reason or another, we begin to wake up a little bit, to lift the nose from the ground and notice that spiritual light and that spiritual atmosphere as real constituents of our human world; then, the whole situation is changed. Our horizon is widened, our experience is enormously enriched, and at the same time our responsibilities are enlarged. For now we get an entirely new idea of what human beings are for, and what they can achieve: and as a result, first our notions about life, our scale of values, begins to change, and then we do.

Evelyn Underhill
From *The Spiritual Life*

All around lie petals
slowly fallen,
leaves that have dropped,
flower heads spent.
A thrush stays just long enough
to say "Goodnight"
and then flies on.
In the garden there is peace,
an air of stillness
unknown in daylight hours.
Leaf and blossom hang together,
tease our memories.
All around a sense of hush.
Blackbirds sing their lullaby
a choir of Nature's own rare quality.
To the west the sun
is setting.
A slowly rolling band of red
then pink that fades
against a striking branch.
A tree of beauty,
it stands majestically against the sky line
then fades away.
It too has gone
until another day.
Lights begin to twinkle
where children sleep.
Cats are out. A walker walks
with stick and dog for company.
Windows close.
Another day awaits.

Judith Lewis
Evening
From her first collection: *Pictures painted in poetry*

Eternity is man's ultimate goal, and the main function of our present life is not merely its enjoyment, so far as possible for its own sake, but also growth in character, by means of the material conditions of life, so that men may be better able to reach their final goal beyond this life. Without this eternal perspective it is impossible to get right our priorities in this world. The secular is not diminished in importance. On the contrary it is the only means whereby we can be in communion with God in this world, and it is the only means whereby men can grow into maturity and so be made ready for eternal life. This perspective of eternity gives heightened importance to and thus heightened concern for the affairs of this world. 'The Saints' Everlasting Rest' may sometimes be used as an escape from the ugly realities of this world. But it should be not only the inspiration behind individual spirituality but also the stimulus behind legislative reform, social endeavour and political action. Seen in this light, this world becomes not merely an end in itself but a preparation for a larger and more final goal. To deny this larger goal, or to ignore its importance is to pervert a true perspective. It is the *trahison des clercs* of the twentieth century.

Hugh Montefiore
From *An Eternal Perspective*

There is an end to grief
Suddenly there are no more tears to cry
No hurt nor break now
But mute acceptance of what will be
Knowing that each move for good or ill
Must fit the whole
Past comprehension
Yet trusted in the design
This way lies peace

Brenda Lismer
On Acceptance

There is nothing in the world of which I feel so certain. I have no idea what it will be like, and I am glad that I have not, as I am sure it would be wrong. I do not want it for myself as mere continuance, but I want it for my understanding of life. And moreover 'God is love' appears to me nonsense in view of the world He has made, if there is no other.

William Temple
On Eternal Life

May you listen to your longing to be free,
May the frames of your belonging be large enough for the dreams of
     your soul;
May you arise each day with a voice of blessing whispering in your
     heart that something good is going to happen to you;
May you find a harmony between your soul and your life;
May the mansion of your soul never become a haunted place;
May you know the eternal longing that is at the heart of time;
May there be kindness in your gaze when you look within;
May you never place walls between the light and yourself;
May your angel free you from the prisons of guilt, fear,
     disappointment and despair;
May you allow the wild beauty of the invisible world to gather you,
     mind you and embrace you in belonging.

John O'Donohue
From *Eternal Echoes: Exploring the Hunger to Belong*

I think of death as a glad awakening from this troubled sleep which we call life; as an emancipation from the world which, beautiful though it be, is still a land of captivity: as a graduation from this primary department into some higher rank in the hierarchy of learning.

Lyman Abbott

As every flower fades and as all youth
departs, so life at every stage,
so every virtue, so our grasp of truth
blooms in its day and may not last forever.
Since life may summon us at every age
be ready, heart, for parting, new endeavour.
Be ready bravely and without remorse
to find new light that old ties cannot give.
In all beginnings dwells a magic force
for guarding us and helping us to live.

Serenely let us move to distant places
and let no sentiments of home detain us.
The Cosmic Spirit seeks not to restrain us
but lifts us stage by stage to wider spaces.
If we accept a home of our own making,
familiar habit makes for indolence.
We must prepare for parting and leave-taking
or else remain the slaves of permanence.

Even the hour of our death may send us
speeding on to fresh and newer spaces,
and life may summon us to newer races.
So be it, heart: bid farewell without end.

Hermann Hesse
From *The Glass Bead Game*

A single life is not much material from which to try to understand something so vastly complex as the world and yet it is all that we have – this brain, this body, this pair of eyes and ears, this very limited experience bounded by genes and capacities and knowledge.

It is with this limited instrument that whatever we understand by meaning must be appreciated and assessed. Just as God, in the Christian tradition, is mediated to us by one human being – Jesus – so life is mediated to us by the particularity of one life – our own. Perhaps it is the particularity which gives the experience such intensity, like a glass focusing the rays of the sun.

Monica Furlong
From *Bird of Paradise*

In the experience of the arts (listening to music, looking at a picture) or when enjoying the view of a wide and various landscape, or during certain moments of tranquillity and happiness in the infinitely diverse experience of human love, the mind seems not to be doing anything at all – it is certainly not pursuing a series of verbal thoughts, it is simply attending in quietness and joy to what is in front of it. It is this faculty of the mind to attend, without one thought giving way to another, simply to be held, that is the characteristic feature of contemplation. Practically everyone is familiar with it. It is the commonest, wisest, safest way into God. The mystics of the great religions were people who were specially gifted with this mental aptitude and cultivated it according to their understanding of God.

During the contemplation of a work of art or while listening to a melody, the effort to understand relaxes and the soul simply delights itself in the beauty which it divines...or perhaps a memory, a word, a line of Dante...shooting up from the obscure depth of our soul, seizes hold of us, recollects and penetrates us. After this experience we know no more than we did but we have the impression of understanding a little something that before we hardly knew...

It is by poetry and penetrating beyond it, by music and penetrating beyond it, that the soul catches a glimpse of the splendour on the other side of the grave, when an exquisite poem brings tears to the eyes, these tears are not proof of excessive pleasure. They are, rather a demand of the soul which longs to seize immediately on this very earth – the paradise revealed to it.

J. Neville Ward
From *The Use of Praying*

AFTERWORD – I

This vision of an ultimate state of affairs in which all is well is a hope. But it is a hope that is witnessed to not only by the Christian faith but by the practical example of countless millions of people, of all faiths and none, who live lives with great courage. For they seem to have an intuitive sense that something vastly important is at stake in all this human travail. In old fashioned language, what is at stake is the making of our eternal souls.

Richard Harries
From *Questioning Belief*

AFTERWORD – II

I don't want to live in vain – make me live for something – I'm no hero. I don't really have whatever it is that makes a hero. But I don't want to be a coward. I don't want to be afraid when the time comes for courage arrives. Let me do something. Let me do it in my own quiet unheroic way. If I can just be remembered as being a good man, as being a distinct and different man, I will feel that I did not waste my life. If I feel that my living here, that the very fact that I existed and lived on earth, meant something to someone, I will be happy. Let me be remembered by someone. Let me help someone – don't permit me to just exist as another human being. Make me live. I don't want to live in vain.

Henri Nouwen
From: *Student Prayers – Making All Things New*

AFTERWORD – III

Forgive what we have been
Help us to amend what we are
And direct what we shall be

From *Prayers of Penitence*
Common Worship, Order I

AFTERWORD – IV

Jesus, as Julian of Norwich, Rembrandt and Henri Nouwen assure us – is both a blessing Father and a caressing Mother, who sees with the eyes of the heart and who, despite our weaknesses and anger, sits completely relaxed, smiling, with a face like a marvellous symphony.

That symphony, which is always evident in God's face, is the future to which all of us, and our earth itself, can look forward. Thus, given that we live under a smiling, relaxed, all-forgiving and all-powerful God, we too should relax and smile, at least once in a while, because irrespective of anything that has ever happened or will ever happen, in the end, 'all shall be well and all shall be well and every manner of being shall be well.'

Ronald Rolheiser
Sustaining ourselves in the spiritual life
From *Seeking Spirituality*

Coda

Dictionaries give two definitions of a 'Coda.' The musical one speaks of it as being something added at the end of a work, sometimes to finalise it, but sometimes, as in the case of Mozart, Haydn and especially Beethoven, to introduce an entirely new theme. It would be impertinent of me indeed to attempt to do the latter, and there is no place for it.

The literary one however speaks of the 'Coda' as rounding off the work, though independent of it. This at least I can attempt to do.

To take the concept of a symphony as a model of the individual's progress through life is imaginative enough. To deal with each of its movements by the quotations in this volume, from sources familiar and less so, is a mark of deep spiritual perception and insight. This is a 'Spiritual Symphony' which strikes deep chords, sympathetic resonances, in the mind and heart of the reader.

Symphony of Life can of course be used as a resource to dip into and find inspiration from, just as sometimes one part of a symphony can give this. But as a symphony needs to be listened to in the entirety of its progress, so this work deserves to be listened to, to be read, heard and absorbed from cover to cover. It is a deeply rewarding journey for which I for one am very grateful.

Bishop John Dennis
August 2009
Winchester

Acknowledgements

The editor would like to register her deep gratitude to:

Tim Ball, Director of Music, Tormead School, Guildford, for advice and guidance on the musical terms used in this book

Roger Gilroy for his brilliant photographic skills, which, together with the work of the Design Team at Diadem Books, have produced a very pleasing cover.

Charles H. Muller and colleagues @ Diadem Books for all their patience, tolerance and courtesy during the production of this work – without whose help, this book would never have come to fruition.

The editor would like to thank all those who have given permission to include extracts in this anthology as indicated below. The compiler and publishers have made every endeavour to trace the copyright owners of each extract. There do, however, remain a small number of short extracts for which the source is unknown to the compiler and publisher. We apologise for this and would be glad to hear from the copyright owners of these extracts so that due acknowledgement can be made in all future editions.

Canterbury Press for permission to quote from *The Coming of God* by Maria Boulding.

Caxton Publishing Group for permission to reprint *Kneeling* by R.S.Thomas, from *Thousand Years of Spiritual Poetry,* edited by Fiona Pagett, 2003.

Continuum for permission to quote from *To Heal a Fractured World,* Chapter 20, Dreams and Responsibilities by Rabbi Jonathan Sacks.

Continuum for permission to quote from *Celebrating Life—Faith Found –* by Rabbi Jonathan Sacks

HarperCollins: for permission to quote from *The Case Against God* by Gerald Priestland, pub.1984, reproduced by kind permission of HarperCollins Publishers Ltd.

HarperCollins: for permission to quote from *My Ascent of Mont Blanc* by Henriette D'Angeville, pub. 1992.

Hodder & Stoughton for permission to quote from *Final Reflections: A Religious Outlook for Modern Man* by Raynor C. Johnson

Hodder & Stoughton for permission to quote from J.H. Oldham – Introduction to Chapter 6 of *Nurslings of Immortality* by Raynor C.Johnson.

Hodder & Stoughton for permission to quote from *The Spiritual Life* by Evelyn Underhill.

Hodder & Stoughton have no objection to the compiler and publishers of *Symphony of Life* quoting from Chapter IV: Sustaining Ourselves in the Spiritual Life, from *Seeking Spirituality* by Ronald Rolheiser, but such permission is given at the compiler and publisher's own risk.

Hodder & Stoughton have no objection to the compiler and publishers of *Symphony of Life* quoting from Chapter II: The Current Struggles with Christian Spirituality, from *Seeking Spirituality* by Ronald Rolheiser, but such permission is given at the compiler and publisher's own risk.

Hodder & Stoughton have no objection to the compiler and publishers of *Symphony of Life* quoting from Chapter I: What is Spirituality? From *Seeking Spirituality* by Ronald Rolheiser, but such permission is given at the compiler and publisher's own risk.

Hodder & Stoughton for permission to quote a short passage from *Devout Sceptics: Conversations on Faith and Doubt – (Bel Mooney talking to Joanna Trollope),*
Copyright 2003, Bel Mooney, first published in Great Britain in 2003 by arrangement with the BBC.

Lion Hudson plc for permission to quote *Uphill* by Christina Rossetti from the Lion Christian Poetry Collection.

Little Brown for permission to use material from Sarah Anderson's Introduction to *The Virago Book of Spirituality.*

Lutterworth Press for permission to quote from A *Prayer for Quiet Hearts* by George Appleton, from *One Hundred Personal Prayers Old and New.*

Oxford University Press: for permission to reprint a short extract by W.R.Inge, from *A Diary of Readings* by John Baillie.

Oxford University Press: for permission to reprint a passage by Philip Gilbert Hamerton from *A Diary of Readings* by John Baillie.

Random House: for permission to reprint a short passage from *Gift from the Sea* by Anne Morrow Lindbergh, published by Chatto & Windus, reprinted by permission of The Random House Group Ltd.

Random House: for permission to reprint a short passage from *Waiting for the Mountain* by Charles Handy, published by Hutchinson. Reprinted by permission of The Random House Group Ltd.

Random House: for permission to reprint a second short passage from *Gift from the Sea* by Anne Morrow Lindbergh, published by Chatto & Windus. Reprinted by permission of The Random House Group Ltd.

Random House: extract from *Gift From The Sea* by Anne Morrow Lindbergh, copyright c.1955, 1975 renewed 1983, by Anne Morrow Lindbergh. Used by permission of Pantheon Books, a division of Random House, Inc.

Random House: for permission to reprint a short passage from 'A Blessing' from *Eternal Echoes* by John O'Donohue, published by Bantam Press. Reprinted by permission of The Random House Group Ltd.

Society of Authors as the literary representative of the Estate of Rosamond Lehmann for permission to quote from *The Swan in the Evening* by Rosamond Lehmann.

Society for Promoting Christian Knowledge for permission to quote from *The Epilogue of Questioning Belief* by Rt. Rev Richard Harries.

Society for Promoting Christian Knowledge for permission to quote from *True Prayer* by Kenneth Leech.

Society for Promoting Christian Knowledge for permission to quote from *Selections from BBC Radio 4's Prayer for the Day* by James Whitbourn.

Society for Promoting Christian Knowledge for permission to quote from *Prayer and Music* by Jeremy Begbie, from the collection entitled *Perspectives on Prayer,* edited by Fraser Watts.

Society for Promoting Christian Knowledge for permission to quote from *Questioning Belief* by Rt. Rev Richard Harries.

Temple Lodge Publishing for permission to quote from *Rudolf Steiner* by Roy Wilkinson, edited by Paul Harris: *An introduction to his spiritual world-view.*

United Agents for permission to reprint extract from *Dancing on the Edge –* copyright Richard Holloway.

Weidenfeld and Nicolson, an imprint of **The Orion Publishing Group London**, for permission to quote from *Through a Window* by Jane Goodall.

Weidenfield and Nicolson, an imprint of **The Orion Publishing Group London,** for permission to quote from *The Quest for God* by Paul Johnson.

W.W.Norton & Co, New York, for permission to quote from *My Life* by Isadora Duncan.

Alphabetical list of contributors

Alphabetical index of first lines

Lightning Source UK Ltd.
Milton Keynes UK
22 November 2010

163248UK00008B/136/P